BLACKFRAMES

Critical Perspectives
on Black Independent Cinema

CELEBRATION OF BLACK CINEMA, INC.

THE MIT PRESS
CAMBRIDGE, MASSACHUSETTS
LONDON, ENGLAND

© 1988 Celebration of Black Cinema, Inc., and The Massachusetts Institute of Technology
Black Frames: Critical Perspectives on Black Independent Cinema is funded by the
Massachusetts Council on the Arts and Humanities, a state agency, and The Commission
of the First Arrival of Africans in Massachusetts.

ISBN 0-262-53080-5

Catalog design: Napoleon Jones-Henderson

Printing by The William Byrd Press, Inc.

All rights reserved. No part of this book may be reproduced or transmitted in any form by
any means, electronic or mechanical, including photocopying and recording, or by any
information storage or retrieval system without permission in writing from the publishers.

FOUNDER'S STATEMENT

Film is a powerful medium, able to evoke emotions, shape ideas, and potentially effect attitudes and behavior. Filmmaking is a complex, time-consuming, and expensive undertaking. For the independent filmmaker, the hurdles of production are followed by the uncertainties of distribution and exhibition. For the black filmmaker, patterns of underrepresentation or exclusion continue to prevail. The fact that there is a dynamic community of black, independent filmmakers despite these obstacles presents good reason to celebrate.

My conception for Celebration of Black Cinema was to highlight the breadth and depth of cinematic expression by black film artists. A historical context would be established by inclusion of some early films. Film historians and critics would be included to participate in the dialogue. But the emphasis would be on the contemporary filmmakers, their films, and their personal vision for their work. Of course, film viewers would gain access to films and filmmakers not often available to the public. Since 1981, Celebration of Black Cinema has produced rich cinematic events which have diversified Boston-area offerings while generating increased interest and support for the films and filmmakers in the wider community.

As Celebration of Black Cinema grows and prospers, I would like to thank those who have been instrumental in making it a reality. Michele Furst nurtured my idea by introducing me to the Boston Film/Video Foundation, which co-sponsored the first three festivals. Special thanks to Julie Levinson, who has given generously of her expertise, time and enthusiasm since the beginning, and whose unswerving commitment to the inclusion of black filmmakers is consistent throughout her career as a programmer and educator. Oliver Franklin first whetted my appetite for these films, helped generously the first year, and introduced me to Pearl Bowser, whose second-year programming served substantially to increase interest and support in the following years. She has been a champion of black cinema, and her commitment to the festival since the early stages is a great source of support and pride.

Since 1986, Claire Andrade-Watkins has been directing the festival and has done an outstanding job expanding the scale of the production and increasing the base of support. This publication is clear evidence of the quality of her and Mbye Cham's efforts.

Many thanks to Massachusetts College of Art, which has provided numerous kinds of support since the beginning, including use of it's screening facilities, and continues to offer support into the future, and the Institute of Contemporary Art for providing the second screening site for the fourth and fifth festivals.

Marcia Lloyd
Founder, Celebration of Black Cinema

TABLE OF CONTENTS

FOREWORD, by Claire Andrade-Watkins

INTRODUCTION, by Mbye B. Cham, Claire Andrade-Watkins

IMAGES OF BLACKS IN BLACK INDEPENDENT FILMS:
A Brief Survey, by James A. Snead

THE CULTURAL CONTEXT OF BLACK BRITISH CINEMA,
by Jim Pines

FILM IN ANGLOPHONE AFRICA: A Brief Survey,
by Manthia Diawara

DIASPORA CULTURE AND THE DIALOGIC IMAGINATION: The
Aesthetics of Black Independent Film in Britain, by Kobena Mercer

THOUGHTS ON NOMADIC AESTHETICS AND
THE BLACK INDEPENDENT CINEMA:
Traces of a Journey, by Teshome H. Gabriel

WE DON'T NEED ANOTHER HERO: Anti-Theses on Aesthetics,
by Clyde Taylor

FOREWORD

The publication of **BLACKFRAMES**: Critical Perspectives on *Black Independent Cinema* heralds a pivotal turning point in the evolution and maturation of Celebration of Black Cinema, Inc.'s Boston-based film program on black independent cinema, founded in 1981 by Marcia Lloyd, an artist and Professor at Massachusetts College of Art.

Although distinguished film historians and scholars have always participated in the event, a primary objective since 1986 has been to expand the scope, significance and substance of accompanying support materials and publications on the history, aesthetics, dialogue and documentation of black independent cinema.

Mbye B. Cham, co-editor of this publication, has been a source of inspiration to all of us for his commitment to encouraging the scholarship on black independent cinema, which is clearly represented in this publication. The enthusiastic response and assistance throughout the preparation of **BLACKFRAMES** by its contributors and Mark Rakatansky of the MIT Press have made this arduous task a delight.

Research in London and Ouagadougou, Burkina Faso, for this publication and for our 1988 film program was made possible through a planning grant from the Massachusetts Council on the Arts and Humanities, a state agency. The resulting publication and film program present a well-rounded purview of the history and aesthetics of independent black cinema from Britain, English-speaking Africa and the U.S.

I would like to express my appreciation to the British Council and Gill Henderson, Jayne Pilling and Irene Whitehead of the British Film Institute, Sheila Whittaker of the National Film Theatre, and Parminder Vir, as well as the scholars, filmmakers and workshops in London and the U.S. for sharing their time, knowledge and institutional support with us as we prepared this publication and film program.

On this side of the Atlantic, many thanks to Susan Hartnett, Patricia Jones, Cornelia Carey, Paula Elliot, Klare Shaw and the staff of the Massachusetts Council on the Arts and Humanities who have labored over, advised and encouraged our work over the last eighteen months. For contributing to the panels on aesthetics and history with our invited scholars and Toni Cade Bambara's closing keynote address during the April 1988 event, special thanks to the Massachusetts Foundation for Humanities and Public Policy and Gail Reimer.

Our ability to institutionalize Celebration of Black Cinema as a major Boston-based forum and film program of national and international note is also attributed to support from the Commission on the 350th Anniversary of the Arrival of Africans in Massachusetts, the Boston Arts Lottery Grant Council, the City of Boston's Office of Arts and Humanities and the Mayor's Office of Business and Culture, Massachusetts College of Art, the Massachusetts College of Art Foundation and Stephen Farrell, Emerson College and the Institute of Contemporary Art, and the Boston Public Library.

The labor of making CBC a reality rests with the outstanding efforts of programmers Pearl Bowser and Julie Levinson, publication designer Napoleon Jones-Henderson, video archival producer Barbara Barrow-Murray, Priscilla Forance,

Zubeidah McLeod, Karen Lindsey and the Harrington family.

Last, but by no means least, is the impressively thorough, efficient and conscientious contribution of June Givanni, CBC's European coordinator. Beyond being an absolute delight to work with, June has a rare ability to make complicated transatlantic logistical, research and negotiating tasks seem effortless.

It is our greatest hope and desire that this work will broaden the knowledge and public awareness of the history, contemporary issues and realities of black independent cinema.

Claire Andrade-Watkins

Co-editor BLACKFRAMES
Director/President
Celebration of Black Cinema, Inc.

INTRODUCTION

This collection of original essays by noted critics and scholars of African descent offers a rare global and systematic examination of the particularities as well as the commonalities of the history, the context and the aesthetics of black independent film practice in "Anglophone" Africa, the United States and Britain.

The emergence in recent years of a significant corpus of highly acclaimed films by people of African descent in different parts of the world heralds the dawn of a new phase in the history and development of film as a medium of creative, cultural and political expression.

Simultaneously building and shifting away from the groundwork of black world filmmakers of an earlier generation, recent film practice and thought of black people in Africa, the United States, Britain and other parts of the globe are reshaping film and pushing it deeper and deeper into newer and hitherto unexplored thematic and formal territories.

Central to this concerted, multifaceted and by no means uniform project of redefinition is a studied awareness of self, rooted in individual and collective memory, vision and aspirations, as well as of the other, now decoded and recoded anew.

Such a project is all-embracing: it is artistic, cultural, social and political. Thus, a reading of black independent film practice in Africa, the United States and Britain, in particular, becomes a reading of the imaginative, the cultural and the socio-political experience and challenges of individuals and societies linked by a common heritage and a history of struggle against similar, and, in many cases, the same forces of oppression and domination.

Three essays provide a discussion and analysis of the history and contemporary dynamics of the infrastructure of black independent film production, distribution and exhibition in the United States, Britain and "English-speaking" Africa. Further, these essays offer a critical account of the general characteristics, tendencies and subject matter of the respective film practices.

James Snead's essay, "Images of Blacks in Black Independent Film: A Brief Survey," traces the development of African-American independent film practice in three different yet related phases, the dominant trait and preoccupation of each phase being shaped and influenced by the nature of the prevailing cultural and socio-economic conditions and attitudes.

From the 1918 production *Birth of a Race* to the 1986 popular hit *She's Gotta Have It*, and including the film work of the 1920–1950 period, indelibly stamped by the work of Oscar Micheaux, to the 1950–1986 period with the emergence of individuals such as William Greaves, St. Clair Bourne, and Shirley Clarke, and of the "L.A. and NYU schools," Snead presents a concise account of the continuities and shifts in all dimensions of a film practice which has always had to contend, one way or the other, with the monster of Hollywood and its surrogates. In fact, it is the first film practice to position itself oppositionally to Hollywood's production norms and racist uses of the medium.

Snead details the genesis and transformations of this posture through the different phases, and what emerges is a pattern that also manifests itself, albeit with different details, in the film practice of Blacks in Britain and, to some extent, Africa. This author's account of the problems, challenges and responses of black independent film production, distribution and exhibition in the United States is echoed in a different context by both Jim Pines on Britain and Manthia Diawara on "Anglophone" Africa. Socio-economic marginalisation and the concomitant denial or difficulty of access to resources vital for film practice are two elements that the black British and African independent filmmaker shares in common with the African-American independent.

A significant convergence of themes among the three film practices clusters around the issues of race, culture and intergroup and interpersonal relations, as well as questions of modes and the language of representation.

As with the approach of Snead's essay, three broad periods in the movement of black independent film in Britain are outlined by Jim Pines' "The Cultural Context of Black British Cinema." The initial period of the 1960s saw the prominence of an interest in feature-length films where the creative treatment of the main subject matter of "race relations" exhibited a good measure of inventiveness in sensitivity and approach to the creative film process itself. Lionel Ngakane's *Jemima and Johnnie* (1964) and Frankie Dymon Jr.'s *Death May Be Your Santa Claus* (1969) are prime examples of this period.

The 1970s, on the other hand, ushered in a second period in which the "fascination with pure cinematic expression" of the first period took a back seat to more documentary, direct and militant explorations of "race relations," identity and intergenerational tension. Horace Ove's landmark 1974 film, *Pressure*, is also cited by Pines as a good example of black British film of this period.

The development of black independent film in Britain in the 1980s is the third period explored in Pines' essay, and is characterized by the emergence of many film and video collectives composed of young, politically aware filmmakers, well versed in film theory.

In the context of "post-multicultural" Britain of the 1980s, the dominant theme of "race relations" of the 1970s is eclipsed by a diversity of the black British experience, articulated in less monolithic terms than before. This broadening of thematic concerns ranges from issues of gender and sexuality from a female perspective to the equally important engagement with form and language of representation. Sankofa's *Passion of Remembrance* (1986) and Black Audio's *Handsworth Songs* (1987) stand out in this respect.

Of course the developments transversing these three broad phases discussed by Pines did not occur in a vacuum. Pines, like Snead, takes great care to consistently provide a clear picture of the sociocultural and political forces influenced by and in turn influencing these developments. This author also provides useful insights into the nature and orientation of film work by Blacks outside of the workshop circuit, i.e., the quasi-commercial sector.

The development of the quasi-commercial sector mentioned above, and its potential in Africa, constitutes the focus of Manthia Diawara's survey of film in English-speaking Africa. The most comprehensive survey to date of film practice in "Anglophone Africa," Diawara's essay explains the factors responsible for the relative poverty of feature-film production in "Anglophone" Africa—factors similar to, if not the same as, those identified by Snead and Pines. He continues on to present an overview of the various film infrastructures, facilities and equipment—governmental and private—in Zimbabwe, Ghana, Kenya, Tanzania and Nigeria.

Historically, film production in these countries tended to be in the documentary format, which developed from the colonial government Film Units where the documentary tradition of Grierson was the norm. That colonial documentary dominance is often cited as a reason to explain the comparatively low level of feature film in Anglophone Africa. However, as Diawara points out, signs of change in this situation are evident in Ghana and Nigeria, where the bulk of feature-film production is surfacing. Although such signs are not yet visible in countries like Zimbabwe and Kenya, these countries do have the resources to challenge the Ghana-Nigeria dominance.

Diawara devotes the major part of his essay to discussing and analysing the plot, themes and styles of the work in Ghana of Kwaw Ansah (*Love Brewed . . . in the African Pot, Heritage*), Nigeria's Ola Balogun (*Black Goddess, Ajani-Ogun, Aiye, Orun Mooru*), and Eddie Ugboma (*The Mask, Death of a President*). Of particular interest is Diawara's discussion of the modes of interaction between film and traditional Yoruba canons of art, especially the influence of traditional Yoruba theatre on film by Nigerians. He refers to the link between African literature and film, and the increasing involvement in film of prominent writers such as Wole Soyinka and Ngugi wa 'Thiong'o. Their involvement reinforces, in a way, one of the pillars of post-esthetic discourse presented by Clyde Taylor in his essay in this collection.

Taken together then, the surveys by Snead, Pines and Diawara present a vivid picture of the historical development and current trends in black world film practice. Details from this picture on the nature and implications of the social, political, cultural and economic context of this film practice also emerge. While the nature of the forces that account for differences may differ in detail, there is a wide area of convergence among the three film practices.

Perhaps it is this high degree of convergence that accounts in large measure for the highly pronounced similarity of views on aesthetics and related questions expressed in the three essays by Kobena Mercer, Teshome Gabriel and Clyde Taylor. Their effort to lay the foundation for the construction of an appropriate critical practice capable of explaining more completely the nature of black film practice rests on the argument that any such construction must be based solidly on materials supplied primarily by the black film practice in all its dimensions: artistic, cultural, social, political and economic. Hence, their unqualified rejection of a wholesale, uncritical and uninterrupted appropriation or imposition of hegemonic a priori notions of criticism developed from or inordinately dependent on mainly Western canons, genres and traditions. Break, delink, disengage, decenter, demolish, deterritorialize, decode, decolonize, deconstruct, recode, reconstruct, revise, liberate, free up, open up, surpass— these are key leitmotifs in the project undertaken by Mercer, Gabriel and Taylor, who expose the impotence and negative implications of dominant Western critical thinking vis-a-vis black film practice, while at the same time reflecting on and proposing possible constituent categories and elements of appropriate black critical practice. In contrast to many dominant Western critical paradigms which are presented here as rigid and dogmatic, black critical practice is conceptualized as dialogic, nomadic and transient.

In his essay "Diaspora Culture and the Dialogic Imagination: The Aesthetics of Black Independent Film in Britain," Kobena Mercer examines the recent work of black British filmmakers and identifies two main tendencies, which he describes as monologic and dialogic. Underlying the monologic tendency in black British filmmaking is a rather uncritical embrace of and dependency on the language and codes of the dominant culture to simply convey a content and subject matter designed to contest racist stereotypical portraits of black people. This is "dependent expressivity" and is an instance of cultural mimicry and neo-colonial surrender, even though works in this category share similar thematic concerns—especially the politics of racism—with works in the other categories.

On the other hand, the dialogic tendency is characterized by a highly pronounced concern with the politics of representation as well as the politics of racism. This work interrupts dominant language and codes, intervenes on the level of film form and enters into critical dialogues with these, equipped with the resources of the full range of its black British experience. Exploring and exploiting "the creative contradictions of the clash of cultures by critically appropriating elements from the master-codes of the dominant culture and creoliz[ing] them, disarticulating given signs and re-articulating their symbolic meaning otherwise," the work in this category represents an instance of what Mercer labels as "carnival" or "creole" aesthetics.

Given the historical and cultural realities of black people in Britain, especially the third generation black British, "whose blackness is thoroughly imbricated in Western modes and codes," Mercer argues that the best possibilities for an appropriate critical language for black British film practice are located in the dialogic principle. In his words, " . . .the issue is not the expression of some lost origin or some uncontaminated essence in black film language, but the adoption of a critical 'voice' that promotes consciousness of the collision of cultures and histories that constitutes our very conditions of existence." Critical dialogism is a project in de-territorialization, decolonization and reconstruction, and as such, it shares much of the principal thrust of Third Cinema, one of whose main exponents, Teshome Gabriel, has now embarked on a project to develop the notion of travelling aesthetics as a key component and a novel re-articulation of the concept of Third Cinema.

In both approach and substance, Teshome Gabriel captures and articulates the notion and spirit of nomadism in his essay, "Thoughts on Nomadic Aesthetics and the Black Independent Cinema: Traces of a Journey." Adopting a refreshingly original approach by crossing generic boundaries and integrating myth, poetry, narrative, interviews and direct and indirect references to secondary sources and photographs, Gabriel's essay readily embodies a cardinal principle of nomadic thought that "all life, experience and existence is without frontiers or boundaries." This central principle, among others, shapes their world view—their conception of reality and fantasy, of time and space—which privileges notions such as ceaselessness, vastness, limitlessness, tentativeness, incompleteness. Gabriel appropriates these concepts and related ideas from the practice and thoughts of the nomads, especially their ideas on art, and adopts and develops them into a fluid system that he relates to the film practice of black world independent filmmakers, much of whose work exhibits, consciously or not, traits of nomadic aesthetics.

This system rejects the notion of "otherness," and proposes, instead, to deal with black film as a new emergent practice with its "own discrete identity, evolving its own axis," and operating in a free open space outside the rigid confines of the Hollywood-Other polarity. In this liberated space, generic boundaries are demolished as the filmmaker, like the nomad, shuttles freely and confidently between documentary, travelogue, experimental and narrative fiction: hence the label "travelling aesthetics."

Integrally tied into this system is also the concept of "the mask as screen," which Gabriel proposes as an effective means of restructuring our film viewing habits. This concept also articulates the idea of the black film as performance, where performer (i.e., film)-audience barriers are broken down and fused in ways that allow interaction "both with the screen and other members of the audience." Kobena Mercer identifies the same element in his analysis of the "carnivalising strategies" evident in the black British film *Territories*.

Conceptualizing aesthetics as a woman— " . . .the concept of 'female' represents that which both nurtures humankind and that which inspires and engenders aesthetic expression"—Gabriel presents a succinct poetic definition of nomadic cinema as observed from the work of filmmakers such as Larry Clarke, Menelik Shabazz, Julie Dash, Gaston Kabore and many others whose work also form the basis for Clyde Taylor's argument for a postesthetic reconstructive critical discourse.

In his essay, "We Don't Need Another Hero: Anti-Theses on Aesthetics," Taylor advocates a radical "break from the repressive doctrine of aesthetics" which is ethnologocentric and Western par excellence [" . . .all aesthetics are Western"], and proposes at the same time "the development of postesthetic creative practice and interpretation." At first glance, Taylor's argument may seem to challenge and even reject the notions of critical dialogism and nomadic cinema as presented by Mercer and Gabriel, respectively, but a close reading of the spirit and the constituent elements of postesthetic practice will reveal the strong ties that bind all three together and the ways in which all three talk to and comment on each other.

Like critical dialogism and nomadism, postesthetic critical practice proposes to construct a model "based on a reorganization of knowledge around and by means of the given text," which is " . . .freed of specious autonomy" and " . . .opened [up] to intercommunication with other texts and to the significations of everyday life." In fact, Taylor's indictment of the Black Aesthetic of the 1960s—its historical and necessary contributions notwithstanding—is based on the latter's concept of the semi-autonomous nature of " . . .cultural production apart from social and material production," and its " . . .fascination with images of perfect and static essences." Postesthetic practice spurns boundaries of any kind and puts a premium on socio-political interpretations over purely formalist ones. Interdisciplinary in nature—politics, sociology, economics, reconstructive Black Studies are integral parts of its model—it is also dialogic, for " . . .a major commitment of postesthetic analysis is the process of transcultural and transideological recoding by which meaning and explanatory power are recouped from dominant paradigms." Postesthetics also incarnates the spirit of nomadism: "The 'post' in postesthetics acknowledges its platform for the assemblage of reconstructive knowledge as inevitably transitory, to be surpassed . . .by more powerful and humane modes of explanation."

This collection is to be seen as part of a steady trickle, since the 1970s, of critical studies and discussions which attempt to describe, analyze and even offer projections on those forces—historical and contemporary, internal as well as external—that have in various ways shaped and influenced the character and make-up of black world independent cinema. Far from being a parochial and narrow-minded excursion into what some others might or do, indeed, consider deformed Euro-American clones, the most accomplished of these studies have proposed and utilized effectively appropriate historical as well as critical approaches to place black world independent cinema not only in its respective contexts, but also in the context of a Third Worldwide cinema practice that aims to mould this art form in ways that confer on it a new mission and a new perspective designed to work in and promote the interests of historically oppressed and exploited individuals and societies. *BlackFrames* opens up new space in this ongoing project of decolonization and self-definition.

Editors:

Mbye B. Cham
Associate Professor
African Studies and Research Program
Howard University

Claire Andrade-Watkins
Assistant Professor
Film Department
Emerson College

IMAGES OF BLACKS IN BLACK INDEPENDENT FILMS: A Brief Survey

James A. Snead

I. Black Independent Filmmakers: The First Generation

Even in the infancy of motion pictures, it was obvious that film, as a new way of perceiving reality, opened up entirely new perceptual possibilities, giving the eye an augmented sense of visual mastery over its surroundings, preserving events in motion for a seemingly unlimited number of future replays, performing a wide variety of functions: educational, propagandistic, recreational, aesthetic. Some idealists—Sergei Eisenstein and Charles Chaplin among them—even thought that film would ultimately bring about a radical improvement in human understanding and communication.

It is one of the bitter ironies of American history, then, that motion picture technology, with its singular potential for good or evil, grew to perfection during the same time period (1890–1915) that saw the systematic, determined, and almost hysterical persecution and defamation of blacks and other minority groups. Early American films depended unthinkingly on theatrical precursors, propagating racial caricatures borrowed from the popular vaudeville and minstrel shows. Black skin (often represented by black-faced whites) came to be linked with servile behavior and marginal status. The repeatability of movies—otherwise a virtue of the medium—offprinted false racial models from celluloid onto mass consciousness again and again; real viewers came to expect unreal blacks both on the screen and in the real world. Film became a hindrance rather than an aid to racial understanding, and in many cases (most notoriously *Birth of a Nation*—1915), served as a tool of the prevailing segregationist and white supremacist dogma.

Given this background, it does not seem unreasonable to connect the birth of black independent cinema with two portentous events in the year 1896 that made black independent films not only possible but inevitable. On April 23 of that year in New York, Thomas Edison demonstrated a major leap in film technology. No longer satisfied with his primitive "Kinetoscope" (which could only accomodate one viewer at a time), Edison introduced large-screen projection, an innovation that would allow movies for the first time to reach a mass audience.[1] And on May 18, less than one month later, the U.S. Supreme Court gave Constitutional assent to segregation in the *Plessy vs. Ferguson* decision, which endorsed "separate but equal" facilities for blacks and whites—a decision not to be reversed until *Brown vs. Board of Education* in 1954. Edison's promotion of movies to a communal (and no longer private) experience, the Supreme Court's division of this potential communality into black and white segments, and the growing resentment by blacks at their remorselessly negative images in mainstream features: All these factors inevitably encouraged and necessitated the first generation of black independent filmmakers.

The term "independent film" must, of course, be used with a great deal of cir-

---

James A. Snead
Associate Professor of English and Film Studies
University of Pittsburgh

cumspection, especially if, as is often the case, it is polemically contrasted with "Hollywood" (therefore "dependent"?) productions. If "dependence" has traditionally meant access to Hollywood's substantial financial resources, its skilled technicians and advanced film technologies, and its ready-made distribution and marketing networks, then for many black and white filmmakers, "dependence" has been something to be desired rather than scorned. In addition, even the so-called "independent" sector customarily (particularly in recent years) depends upon the keenly sought support of private investors, foundations, and public grants. One can declare one's independence, but in film—a particularly collective and capital-intensive art form—true independence is hardly attainable, even in the most modest productions.

Yet for many independent filmmakers, the word "independent" does not refer to any such one-dimensional version of economic self-reliance. Rather, the relative financial constraints under which independent filmmakers—and particularly black filmmakers—have operated for decades have often led to a certain aesthetic and creative privilege. Vincent Canby's comment in the *New York Times* on Warrington Hudlin's *Black at Yale* represents a not uncommon misunderstanding about the nature of independent film: *"Black at Yale* is a film limited only by the resources of money and time available to the director."[2] Yet it is by no means clear that more "money and time" would have made *Black at Yale* a proportionately better film. Indeed what Canby refers to as "limitations" (which Hudlin's film shares with practically the entire line of black independent films since William Foster's *The Pullman Porter* in 1910) precisely delineate the strength of the independent film. Without the incessant and confining restraints of box-office considerations, studio agenda, and censoring boards, the range of artistic choice in independent films is potentially *widened*, rather than *restricted*.

Because of, rather than *in spite of*, limited budget and screening opportunities, the adept filmmaker can exploit his or her marginal position to present the kinds of statements and images which can go against prevailing rules and codes. Such a filmmaker can choose to refute, to parody, or merely to copy Hollywood models—as in the cases of *A Black Sherlock Holmes* (ca. 1918), produced by the (mainly white) Ebony Film Company, or *By Right of Birth* (1921), produced by George P. and Noble Johnson's Lincoln Motion Picture Company. Yet even such derivative films by black independent companies were not just slavish sepia replicas of white Hollywood; they often involved subtle, even inadvertent, critiques of white America's racial politics. Real-world *disparities* between white archetype and black copy intrude, often explicitly, to uncover unspoken political realities. Indeed, for many such films, their very technical and financial inferiority to Hollywood productions exposes the very real-life disparities between the races generally that the film's "apolitical" plot is trying to conceal.

The "independence" of the black filmmakers in the '20s was not a deliberate choice but was enforced—in every sense—by the highest legal tribunal of the land. In the first four decades of American film history, black independent films were a product of a separationist environment, which also accounted for their major market opportunity—pleasing a growing but cinematically underrepresented black audience.

The first generation of black independent filmmakers was active, albeit with uneven success, from about 1910 until the late 1930s. William Foster's Photoplay Company had produced black independent films as early as 1910, but most critics agree that the first major black independent effort was *Birth of a Race* in 1918.

17

Artistically one of the least successful, but one of the most powerful in terms of its political aspirations, *Birth of a Race* arose primarily in opposition to the radically ungenerous and laughably inaccurate depiction of black people in D.W. Griffith's *Birth of a Nation* (1915). To counter Griffith's propaganda, Emmett J. Scott (former secretary to Booker T. Washington) formed the Birth of a Race Company. After three years spent securing patchy and often unreliable funding both from black and white sponsors, Scott managed to turn out *Birth of a Race* (1918). Scott's film matched Griffith's epic in its pretensions, exceeded it in its length, but was woefully inferior to it in almost every other respect. The intended narrative—a comprehensive history of the Negro's past, present, and future, from Africa to America and beyond—was never finished, and the film (as mandated by some of its backers) ended up seeming like a pacifist commentary on the causes of World War One. Unfortunately, this most ambitious but technically and conceptually flawed project only seemed to show that "propagandistic rebuttals to propaganda were not yet feasible, especially from an Afro-American producer."[3]

II Black Independent Filmmakers: 1920–1950

But there were other black artists at work as well. Perhaps because of its idiosyncratic aspirations, the failure of *Birth of a Race* did little to halt the courting of the black audience by other black filmmakers (often financed by white co-producers) and indeed may have spurred on their pursuit of that audience. The '20s helped establish black independent films as viable alternatives to the Hollywood product. Alongside the Ebony Motion Picture Company, which produced films for black audiences but allowed little creative or conceptual input by blacks, there were comparable companies with a high degree of black involvement. The Johnsons' Lincoln Motion Picture Company was one such company which, unlike the older Foster Photoplay Company, achieved a relatively high degree of success in the late teens and into the '20s with its productions *The Trooper of Troop K* (1917), *The Realization of a Negro's Ambition* (1917), and *By Right of Birth* (1921). But the fluid imprecision of the concept "independent" becomes clear when one notes that ultimately both William Foster and Noble Johnson left their own independent production companies for the lure of Hollywood, a kind of career "crossover" that is still common among today's independents.

The Lincoln Company's productions, both under the Johnsons and their successor, Clarence Brooks, tended to emphasize black pride and consciousness, and were often explicitly political, but they were exceptions to the rule. Generally, "black" independent film companies (many of them, such as the Reol Motion Picture Corporation, or the Colored Players Film Corporation, actually organized and financed by whites) gave black audiences an image of a black middle class full of cultured, affluent, and well-mannered families more or less free from racial misery—indeed, an image conforming to the way Hollywood films typically portrayed "normal" whites as living.

The Colored Players Film Corporation is an exemplary case of a black-white joint venture which managed a high level of production integrity in its many films, including *A Prince of His Race* (1926), the temperance piece *Ten Nights in a Barroom* (1926), and perhaps most notably, *Scar of Shame* (1928). *Scar of Shame* certainly ranks among the most technically adept and thematically compelling films of the early black independent period. The film convincingly mixes black urban reference-points (slang, ghetto scenes, dress conventions) with a somewhat melodramatic Hollywood-style "social climbing" plot in which Alvin Hilliard, a middle-class composer, falls in

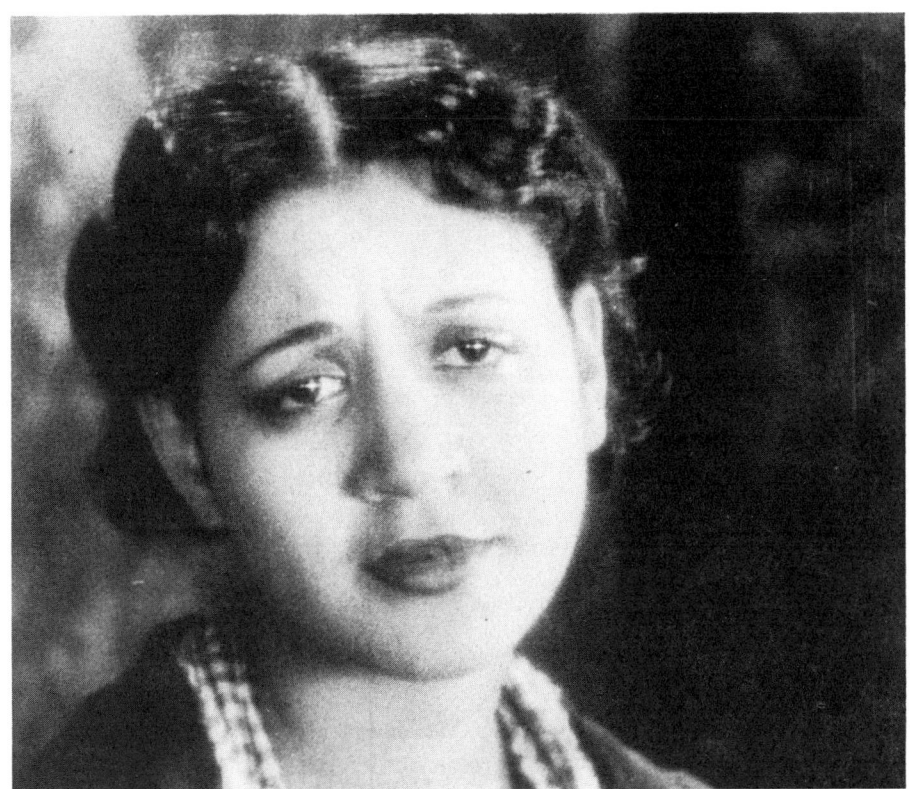

SCAR OF SHAME: Lucia Lynn Moses, courtesy of: The Chamba Educational Film Services Collection

love with Louise, a beautiful lower-class girl. Their rise and eventual demise, far from having anything to do with what Thomas Cripps calls "color-caste snobbery" (if this assertion were true, then one would expect Hilliard's mother to *embrace*, rather than reject, the lighter-toned Louise; in this case, class overrides skin color), is a fairly straightforward parable of class conflict within the black community.[4] The film's iconography (for example, the "book and lamp" motto on the title cards) is often unintentionally ironic, and its symbolism all too frequently leaden, but overall, the film commands and articulates a cinematic vocabulary that sets it apart from any but the most accomplished Hollywood productions of the '20s.

Oscar Micheaux was the dominant personality of this period, and typified better than anyone of this generation the all-around "black independent filmmaker," writing, financing, producing, directing, and distributing his own films. Starting with his first feature *Homesteader* (1919)—based on his autobiographical novel of the same title—he made thirty-three films in thirty-three years. His most provocative films include *Body and Soul* (1924)—which was Paul Robeson's first film, *The Wages of Sin* (1929—now lost), and *God's Stepchildren* (1937).

Even more than with other art forms, the prosperity and even survival of a film will require it to maintain a certain pre-existing status quo. The diversity of Micheaux's

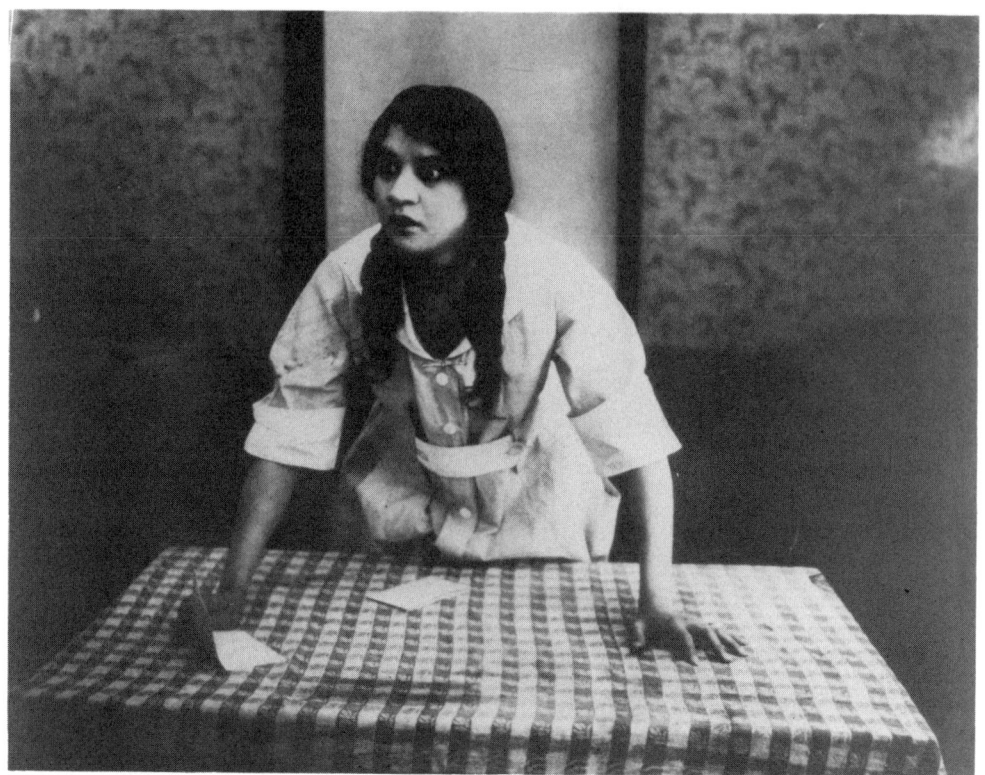

THE HOMESTEADER: Oscar Micheaux, courtesy of: The Chamba Educational Film Service Collection

films makes generalization about them difficult, but one can safely assert that, as with the Johnson brothers, Micheaux did not shy away from politically disturbing topics, even topics that might have offended some black audiences. Yet even in his less controversial films, Micheaux encountered problems that had little to do with politics or ideology. The always insufficient financial backing for his projects led to a sloppy, "single-take" aesthetic, compounded by the often insufficient attention to heavy-handed scripts, badly directed actors, and primitive handling of lighting and camera movement. These deficiencies plagued "race films" generally, and gave Hollywood films a competitive advantage, even among black audiences. By the end of the '20s, Hollywood had already begun to incorporate elements of black culture into highly polished productions such as *Hallelujah!* (1929) and *Hearts in Dixie* (1929), further siphoning off black filmmakers' potential audience. Hence a paradox arose: studio-processed and ill-informed images of blackness seemed more believable than black-sourced but technically amateurish images produced for black audiences by Micheaux and others.

Even apart from purely technical issues, the disappearance of the first generation of black independent filmmakers was hastened both by the Great Depression (which dried up sources of financial support) and by the advent of sound films (which sent the costs of production far beyond what most independents could afford). Most of their films have disappeared as well. The record of these films has been irretrievably damaged: all prints deteriorate with time, and few black independent producers could afford to make replacement copies, so time's effects have censored what even a racist environment could not, and of the hundreds of early black filmprints, only a small fraction survive today.

Despite the large numbers of all-black "race films" produced in the '30s and the '40s, there were only a few remarkable examples of independent black filmmaking in the period. For the most part, with the new resources of sound film, black productions relied on routine musicals or melodramas with little political or social substance. Among the foremost black directors of the '30s was George Randol, who produced and directed (with Ralph Cooper) an independent all-black gangster film called *Dark Manhattan* (1937). The picture became a box-office hit "even though it was difficult to convince the [white] exhibitors that colored people would pay high prices to see their own race on the screen."[5] Million Dollar Pictures, with whom Randol was loosely associated, went on to produce a stream of quality films—mainly offprints of stock studio themes of romance, society, comedy, and crime. Randol's films, such as *Gangsters on the Loose* (1938), *Reform School* (1939), and *While Thousands Cheer* (1940), tended, like their Hollywood counterparts, to skirt controversial issues.

Another prominent black independent filmmaker of this era was Spencer Williams, who often simultaneously served as star, producer, and director. His Amegro Films produced *The Blood of Jesus* (1941) and *Go Down Death* (1944), both examples of allegorical dramas firmly based in rural black religious and poetic traditions. Yet overall, aside from these and a handful of other films (including those of Oscar Micheaux, who had survived the Depression and moved with seeming aplomb into the sound era), the horizontal and vertical monopolization of the film industry by the major studios, combined with the introduction of noted black actors (such as Mantan Moreland, Ethel Waters, and Bill Robinson) into white films, had by the late '40s all but extinguished the early vitality of black independent film.

III Black Independent Filmmakers: 1950–1986

In this, most recent, phase of black independent filmmaking, technological innovations once more have conspired with political developments, but this time with happier results than in the late 1890s. The 1954 desegregation decision that overturned *Plessy vs. Ferguson* began a series of events leading from the Montgomery bus boycotts and the Little Rock crisis through the flourishing of the nationwide Civil Rights Movement and the initiation, in the mid-sixties, of the Black Power movement. Black people attained a greater political and symbolic significance in the American mind than ever before, such that within only a few years their prior images in mainstream Hollywood films were rendered inadequate. Even the pioneering Hollywood "race films" of the late '40s (*Home of the Brave*, *Pinky*, and *Lost Boundaries* in 1949) and the '50s (a series of films, mainly starring Sidney Poitier, between *No Way Out* in 1950 through *The Defiant Ones* in 1958) had begun, in light of the realities of the '60s, to seem sententious at best and condescending at worst. Hollywood was still unable to discern or depict the full spectrum of black American life and culture.

At the same time, technological improvements led to reductions in the price (and just as importantly, the weight) of 16mm camera and synch-sound equipment, which, together with improvements in the quality of film stock, made the 16mm format accessible to filmmakers with low budgets while making their "look" and "sound" acceptable to a broader public. The "New Wave" and *cinema verite* movements gave a certain high-cultural sanction to the use of "real-life" subjects as raw material for independent film, and in many cases blurred the distinction between "documentary" and "fictional" films altogether, creating both an appetite and a system of distribution ("art houses", public television, museums) for filmmaking that did not conform to the visual and narrative principles of Hollywood's "classical realist" tradition.

As a direct result of the Civil Rights Movement, black students began entering university film programs and film schools in large numbers in the '60s, and—in contrast to many earlier black independents—became the politically engaged beneficiaries of a stylistic and technical revolution in the world of film. Skeptical about the ability of the mainstream American film industry to put its house in order, this new generation of black independent filmmakers decided to exploit film's full aesthetic and political potential. They set about *recoding* black skin on screen and in the public realm by revising the contexts and concepts with which it had long been associated. Many of these filmmakers belonged to the black middle class and were formally trained at leading universities and film schools. But, unlike many of their precursors in the '20s and '30s, they insisted on engaging problems that addressed the diverse experience of all segments of the black community.

William Greaves was one of the pioneers of this new movement. Starting out as an actor (he appeared in *Lost Boundaries*), Greaves soon moved into film documentary work with the National Film Board of Canada, and later with the United Nations before becoming Executive Producer of WNET's "Black Journal," a television series that turned out many of the most aggressive and engaged social documentaries of the '60s. Two of his best films, *Still a Brother: Inside the Negro Middle Class* (1968) and *Ali, the Fighter* (1971) indicate Greaves' range, technical acumen, and emotional affinity with the black community. He remains an "independent," even though he has directed and produced Hollywood features as well. Documentary and *cinema verite* formats also attracted Shirley Clarke—best known for *The Connection* (1961), *The Cool World* (1963), and *Portrait of Jason* (1967)—and St. Clair Bourne (also an alumnus of "Black Journal"), whose television documentary *Let the Church Say Amen* (1973) set new standards for films of its kind.

In the '70s, the range and variety of black independent filmmaking expanded, and with it, the extent to which these films proliferated newer, authentic codings for images of black skin. There were more fictional and narrative films, and, in gaining worldwide recognition at Third World and European film festivals, black independent filmmakers now asserted their identity as a distinct and original group primed to contribute significantly to the history of filmmaking. A few independent films, such as Roy Campanella's *Pass Fail* (1978) even thematized the figure of the black independent filmmaker trying to reconcile an artistic mission (which involves breaking away from stereotyped roles) with white institutional demands to compromise or commercialize their recoding efforts. Or, in another example, the opening scenes of Haile Gerima's *Bush Mama* (1977) show black independent filmmakers in conflict with institutional authority. In this case—which was *not* staged— the L.A. Police stop and frisk a group of filmmakers merely *because* they are black men with camera equipment, graphically illustrating the threat felt by the status quo when blacks take control of their own images.

The majority of recent black independent films since the '60s have the feeling of intimate conversations between filmmaker and audience, and deal with issues *within* the black community, without special regard for a theoretical white viewer. Henry Miller's *Death of a Dunbar Girl* (1974) and *Color* (1982) by Warrington Hudlin and

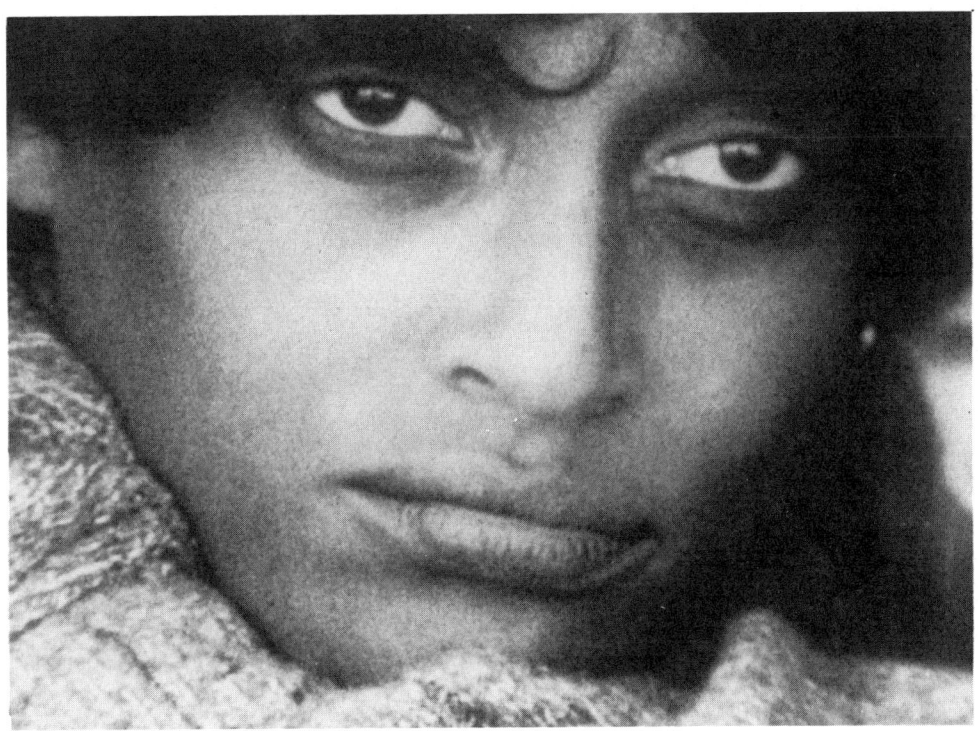

BUSH MAMA: Haile Gerima, courtesy of: Mypheduh Films

Denise Oliver both deal with class and color-caste discrimination more honestly, concisely, and credibly than *Scar of Shame* had in the '20s; *Suzanne, Suzanne* (1982) by James Hatch and Camille Billops emotionally mines, using Bergmanesque techniques, the story of an abused wife and her heroin-addicted daughter trying to compose a post-mortem on their recently dead husband, father, and tormentor—these are themes which the early black independent filmmakers would have treated indirectly, if at all. The viewer achieves, in the best of these films, an understanding of a complex black world from within, rather than caricature of it from without.

An important grouping of this new generation was active in Los Angeles between around 1972 and 1982. Most of these filmmakers were trained at the UCLA film school, but their films protest against the form and content of the tradition they were being taught. Their chief ambition was to rewrite the standard cinematic language of cuts, fades, frame composition, and camera movement in order to represent their own "non-standard" vision of black people and culture. Haile Gerima's *Child of Resistance* (1972) and *Bush Mama*, Larry Clark's *Passing Through* (1977), Ben Caldwell's *I and I: An African Allegory* (1977), and Charles Burnett's *Killer of Sheep* (1977) rank among the virtuoso articulations of this new stylistic sensibility. Julie Dash's *Illusions* (1982), and Alile Sharon Larkin's *A Different Image* (1982) extend the early methods and insights of the mainly male "L.A. School," integrating their unconventional stylistics and thematics with a frankly and refreshingly feminist reading of sexual and racial oppression. In their rejection of that kind of glossy technical sophistication that historically defines Hollywood's "classic realist" cinema, and in their refusal to

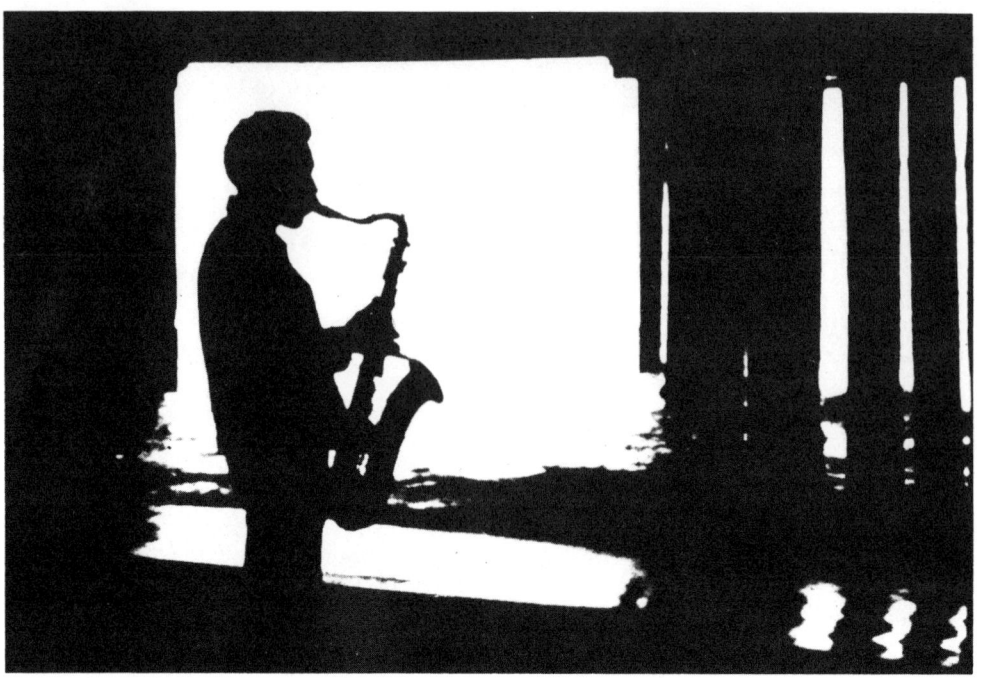

PASSING THROUGH: Larry Clark, courtesy of: Larry Clark

remain on the easy surface of human relationships, L.A.'s black independent filmmakers continue in the '80s to define the possibilities and limits of this second flowering of black independent film.

IV Black Independent Filmmakers: Beyond the '80s

Under the rubric of *entertainment*—and with the help of unprecedented investment in pyrotechnics, special visual effects, and computerized graphics and animation—the Hollywood film industry in the '80s seems determined to suppress sensitivity and three-dimensionality under a veneer of technical gloss. The future of black independent filmmaking will more and more rely on how these filmmakers handle the competitive challenge from an increasingly monopolistic and compelling industry. The mesmerizing visual enchantments of a *Beverly Hills Cop* series or a *Star Wars* trilogy have led to enormous box office success—most notably among black audiences. Yet even box-office breakthroughs by Richard Pryor, Eddie Murphy, or Whoopi Goldberg cannot disguise the fact that blacks are still being portrayed in aberrant and even bizarre roles that are mere descendants of paradigms set by Eddie Anderson, Stepin Fetchit, or Ethel Waters.

Towards the end of the '80s, a younger set of black filmmakers has achieved an unprecedented prominence, but it remains to be seen whether they will retain their prior artistic independence. The point can be illustrated by looking at three of the best recent black independents. Spike Lee's fine series of early films (produced at the NYU Film School), *The Answer* (1980), *Sarah* (1981), *Joe's Bed-Stuy Barbershop: We Cut Heads* (1983), and *She's Gotta Have It* (1986) reveal a quirky yet appealing filmic sensibility and a familiarity with the diverse social and economic condition of black Americans that few filmmakers, white or black, achieve. Mary Neema Barnette's *Sky Captain* (1984) and Reginald Hudlin's *House Party!* (1984) and *Reggie's World of Soul* (1985) share with Lee's films a fluent command of black and white cultural languages, and an insistence on counterposing them in an aesthetic dialectic. Instead of seeing blacks purely in terms of white norms and practices, these films show blacks securely positioned in their own environments, discussing and dealing with their own problems, ignoring or at best belittling the toys and games of the dominant white culture. Yet these directors, among the best of the late '80s, have received substantial attention from Hollywood, and at least two of them are actively engaged in feature film production. It will be interesting to see in the coming years whether the oppositional aesthetics and thematics of their earlier "independent" films can be adapted for mass-market consumption. Some would doubt whether white Americans can ever learn to see blacks and themselves from a black, and not a white, vantage-point. Lee's comedy *She's Gotta Have It* became, despite less-than-ideal production values, a major box office hit across the nation, attracting a considerable white audience. But whether a mass public could assimilate the messages and the methods of as somber a film as *Killer of Sheep* is another question. And one further question remains: should it? Perhaps the greatest challenge for future black filmmakers, independent or not, is to find a way to prevent an imagistic cooptation in which an insincere, ritualized tolerance of recoded images may itself become just another way of keeping blacks out of the picture.

FOOTNOTES

(1) James Monaco, *How to Read a Film: The Art, Technology, Language, History, and Theory of Film and Media* (New York, Oxford University Press, 1981), p. 200.

(2) Quoted in The Black Filmmaker Foundation, *Black Cinema* (New York, 1982), p. 39.

(3) James R. Nesteby, *Black Images in American Films, 1896-1954: The Interplay Between Civil Rights and Film Culture* (New York: University Press of America, 1982), p. 68, and passim, gives an exhaustive treatment of the entire early period of black filmmaking.

(4) Thomas Cripps, *Black Film as Genre* (Bloomington: Indiana Univ. Press, 1978), p. 69.

(5) James Asendio, "History of Negro Motion Pictures," *International Photographer*, January 1940, p. 16.

THE CULTURAL CONTEXT OF BLACK BRITISH CINEMA

Jim Pines

I

The 1980s have been a kind of watershed for Black independent film and video in Britain. With the emergence of a new generation of practitioners whose work reflects a diverse range of thematic and formal concerns, there has been a significant shift not only in terms of accepted notions of "British" film culture, which hitherto ignored the work of Black practitioners, but also in terms of institutional cultural (funding) policy. Through various mechanisms, including productions and associated screenings and representation on key institutional committees, Black film and video independents have been able to revise the cultural agenda in relation to their own cultural and political concerns, as well as in relation to the way in which this intervention necessarily affects the wider society. The "recognition" of this Black presence in the film and television culture has become a new and significant factor, particularly within the more liberal progressive areas of the British cultural scene, which has resulted in marked "adjustments" at the institutional level. However, these developments have not led to the complete radicalisation of the cultural terrain, because Black independent media practitioners to a very large extent are still hamstrung by, and thus are having to continue struggling against, recurrent institutional and cultural marginalisation. In other words, the "dominant" cultural and funding bodies have thus far succeeded only in accomodating certain elements of change, without really altering the fundamental structures in their thinking and in their institutional practices.

Although resistance to exclusion and marginalisation remains high on the agenda, other issues are now emerging into the forefront which are equally vital to the development of the sector, i.e., issues which one might define as Black-specific in orientation—like the development of a genuinely independent Black film culture, and concomitantly the shaping of an expressive film "language" which draws on and addresses in very specific ways particular features of Black cultural experiences. This has led to a number of new tendencies emerging within the sector, such as an interest in formal experimentation, particularly among more theoretically-aware practitioners, and a growing concern with practical matters like distribution and exhibition, which earlier Black practitioners were simply unable to undertake. Indeed, the widening circulation of Black and Third World films in Britain in the past couple of years has opened the possibility for new and more effective means of consolidating important areas of film-related cultural work, mainly, but not exclusively, through the promotion of Black-owned distribution and exhibition networks. Of course more work still needs to be done on audience-building, especially given the fact that many people, Black and white, still tend to approach Black films with a sense of uncertainty at best. But recent experience indicates that this area of cinema is becoming increas-

Jim Pines
freelance writer, London

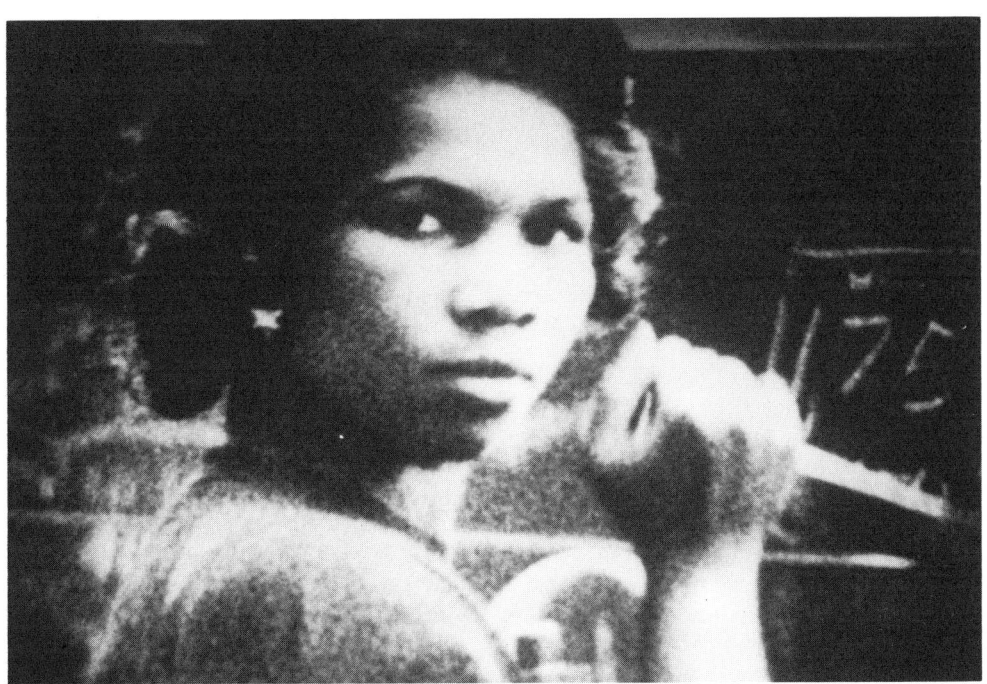

HANDSWORTH SONGS: Black Audio Film Collective, courtesy of: Black Audio Film Collective

ingly "less difficult" or more viable both in a cultural and a (quasi-) commercial sense.

In an important sense, these developments within the Black independent film and video sector in Britain have to be seen against the backdrop of eighties cultural politics, which in terms of Black politics signalled the break with old-style "race relations" and multiculturalism. For many practitioners, the old preoccupation with conventional race-relations motifs had become more or less redundant. The privileging of Black-white relations in the classic "race problem" sense was therefore seriously called into question, as it became patently obvious that this orientation was (is) really inappropriate in the context of "post-multicultural" Britain in the 1980s. The emphasis thus shifted towards a broader, more critical orientation which stresses a completely different set of political and cultural concerns, such as the need to retrieve and re-present Black people's own histories through "archival excavation" (Black historiography), and the importance of deploying motifs which convey a more complex sense of contemporary Black (British) experiences from a Black perspective. Within this framework, "race relations" is strategically re-positioned within a broader set of socio- political and cultural concerns, thus making it possible—for the first time in the British context—to address Black themes without having to directly involve otherwise omnipresent white figures in the narrative.

A good example of this radical departure into new territory is Sankofa's compelling drama *The Passion of Remembrance* (1986), which links together questions of race, class, sexuality, and gender, and explores the way in which these issues relate specifically to Black communities, i.e., relations among Black people, rather than between Blacks and whites per se. In a similar vein, Black Audio Film Collective's documentary *Handsworth Songs*

(1986) takes us along another path of resistance, through the creative blending of archival footage, political reportage, and historical symbolism, and signals a formidable challenge to the British race-relations documentary tradition (which for decades has been immensely effective in promulgating problem-oriented sociological representations of "race" in Britain). These films offer new insights into the nature of the Black experience in post-Imperial Britain, and they also suggest new possibilities in representing Black social, political, cultural, and historical realities which (again) could not have been contemplated in previous decades. These developments challenge critics, theorists, historians, and practitioners interested in the evolution of Black (British) cinema to re-assess old paradigms and to take into fuller account the political and cultural significance of Black-produced (oppositional) imagery in representations of contemporary Britain.

II

Black independent film production in Britain dates back to around the mid-1960s, but it was at least a decade before cultural institutions started to recognise or make provisions for this activity within "official" cultural funding policy. Thus, the handful of Black independents at the time operated in a characteristically entrepreneurial fashion, financing small to modest productions out of their own pockets or by other, more "unconventional" means. For example, Horace Ove's engaging documentary *Reggae* (1970) was financed by a Black independent record producer. In sharp contrast to the situation today, earlier Black independents did not engage in institutional cultural politics to any great extent, preferring instead to remain outside the white-dominated structures which in any case showed no interest in non-white film cultural activity. Even during the mid-1970s, the height of film theory and cultural expansion in Britain (which centred largely around *Screen* magazine and the British Film Institute's regional policy), there was precious little to be heard relating to Black cultural production.

Ironically, this exclusion from the main cultural debates and policy initiatives of that era tended to reinforce a feeling of cultural and creative independence among many Black practitioners. However, it also helped to perpetuate the dangerous notion that Black people were either not seriously engaged in film- and video-related activity, or, if they were, that their work was not relevant to a wider constituency. It was therefore relatively easy for the cultural mandarins and their so-called enlightened clients to turn a blind eye to Black-related cultural matters, despite the fact that much of it actually had a great deal to say about Britain in the sixties and seventies.

Of course these institutional responses were part of a much broader cultural debate which, needless to add, the handful of Black independents at the time did not participate in. Without putting too fine a point on it, this period witnessed a sort of crisis within British film culture, in which the whole field of production, distribution, exhibition, and film cultural theory was being contested. The notion of subsidised independence became one of the central themes in the debates, particularly for those (progressive white) independents wanting to develop their craft outside (or in opposition to) the mainstream industry, and this led eventually to the grant-aided independent sector as we know it today. But because Black independents had no input in these developments, they failed to get an early footing in the organisation of the independent film and video sector. Consequently, they continued to be marginalised, even by the liberal progressive wing of the culture industry.

But whether Black film-making would have developed more rapidly or more prolifically if it had been incorporated into the main independent sector at the time, we shall never know. What does seem clear, however, is that the lack of an organisational base from which to promote their activities prevented Black independents from making a bigger impact on the cultural scene, and this inevitably affected the way in which Black film and video developed through the 1970s. However, it would be a mistake to push this line of argument too far, because in a very real sense the cultural milieu in which Black film and video practitioners lived and worked during the sixties and seventies was largely incompatible with the culture of the white independent sector and its institutional support structure. Although they shared similar problems, such as funding, the white and Black independents did not share the same preoccupation regarding film cultural theory. This was to come in the 1980s, with the emergence of a new generation of Black film/video practitioners well-versed in issues of theory.

Black film-making as an oppositional (cultural) practice refers to the complex relationship between Black-produced imagery and dominant representation. It is more than simply a matter of Black film-makers projecting "positive" images of Black people, although this is an important consideration; it denotes the way in which historically Black-related themes and imagery have been tied inextricably to the exegesis of "official" race relations discourse. Documentary realism is particularly relevant in this context, not only because of its colonial legacy and the fact that it has been the principal form of dominant representations of "race" in Britain, but also because it has had a profound impact on the form and content of Black British films and videos, both documentaries and narrative fiction. This is also one of the ways in which Black films are marked off from other kinds of independent work, because institutionalised "race relations" has a marginalising effect structurally and tends to reinforce rather than ameliorate the "otherness" of the subject—which documentary realism historically and representationally embodies. Within this set of relations, therefore, it has been difficult for Black practitioners to evolve a cinematic approach which is largely unaffected by the determinants of "race relations" discourse or which works outside documentary realism. This is not as negative as it sounds, however, because a closer look at the history of Black films in Britain will reveal numerous instances of film-makers manipulating, if not entirely subverting, the codes of race relations and multiculturalism, and constructing narratives which go some way towards critiquing the "official" discourse, mainly at the level of content, not form.

Nevertheless, it should be stressed that the propensity for creative cinematic expression, in terms of style and content, was strongly evident during a brief period in the early years of Black independent film-making, i.e., prior to the institutionalisation of British "race relations" which would eventually permeate all aspects of racial discourse and representation from the late 1960s onwards. A good example is Lionel Ngakane's allegorical short film *Jemima and Johnnie* (1964), where the "race relations" story is developed cinematically without the narrative being hamstrung by the racial theme. This charming film is one of the earliest attempts to seriously explore the dynamics of British "race relations" in narrative fiction from a Black point of view, and its "re-discovery" several years ago reaffirmed the existence of an interesting history of Black film-making in Britain. The story follows the exploits of two children—one Black, the other white—who happily run off to play together in the streets, their "disappearance" causing the distressed parents to join in the search for them. The film used this simple but effective device to comment on the stupidity of racial intolerance, at a time when racial antagonisms were running high in Britain. The final image of unconditional friendship between the children, in contrast to the adults' uneasy interracial cooperation, struck an optimistic note, invoking the possibility of racial harmony in the face of growing prejudice and suspicion. Despite the "obviousness" of the story situation, the film achieves its effect not so much through the use of a stereotypical (racial) narrative, but as a result of Ngakane's marvellous sense of cinematic expression, which is clearly rooted in a quality of social realism prevalent in the British left-liberal independent film movement during the 1950s-60s.

In a similar vein, though with quite different intentions, Frankie Dymon, Jr.'s "pop fantasy" *Death May Be Your Santa Claus* (1969), constructs a Dantesque narrative centering on a Black hero's imaginary journey through a nightmarish world of political violence, alienation, and eventual self-rediscovery. The film draws heavily on the themes and imagery of sixties cultural politics like Black Power, Che Guevara, the Underground Movement, pop culture, "Flower Power," Vietnam, and so on, which are all worked into the non-realist narrative in a typically iconoclastic manner. Interestingly, the film was inspired by the director's involvement (as an actor) in Jean-Luc Godard's British film *One Plus One*. While Dymon, Jr.'s iconoclasm is largely instinctive and "un-theorized," it nevertheless exemplifies the degree to which early Black practitioners were quite responsive to a wide range of cinematic techniques and practices. Of course this fascination with pure cinematic expression—which in this example touches on the avant-garde—completely disappeared by the early-seventies, though, happily, aspects of it have reappeared in some recent works by the present generation of Black film/video practitioners.

So, from these two quite different examples, we can see how early Black filmmaking was not only inventive in its approach to political (racial) themes, but also sensitive to the creative film process itself. It's also worth mentioning in this context that while a number of the film-makers were trained at the London Film School (now the London International Film School), renowned for its highly motivated students, the majority in fact received no such formal training, but worked in other disciplines like writing and acting. What they all shared in common was an immense enthusiasm for the medium, and a burning desire to extend their creative energies into this otherwise highly expensive art form. Significantly, there was little interest in straightforward documentary forms of film-making, and more in feature-length production with a somewhat commercial or entertainment orientation in mind. This did not mean the abandonment of serious social issues, however, but rather a desire to incorporate these kinds of themes into narrative fiction and on a fairly grand ("serious") scale. Interestingly, the Hollywood entertainment films (especially those with Sidney Poitier) and the European "art movies" both provided useful, albeit contradictory, models.

III

Although Black film-makers started to receive a degree of recognition by the early-1970s, institutional support for Black films remained notably lacking, with only perhaps the occasional race-relations-supported project receiving significant funding from any major institution. However, a turning point came when the British Film Institute's Production Board funded Horace Ove's first feature, *Pressure* (1974), which was also the first British-made feature film by a Black director. It is a classic "race relations" drama which draws on a number of familiar themes, such as the "immigrant problem" and the problem of assimilation, and reworks them into the film's documentary-like fictional narrative. In the context of the 1970s, the story

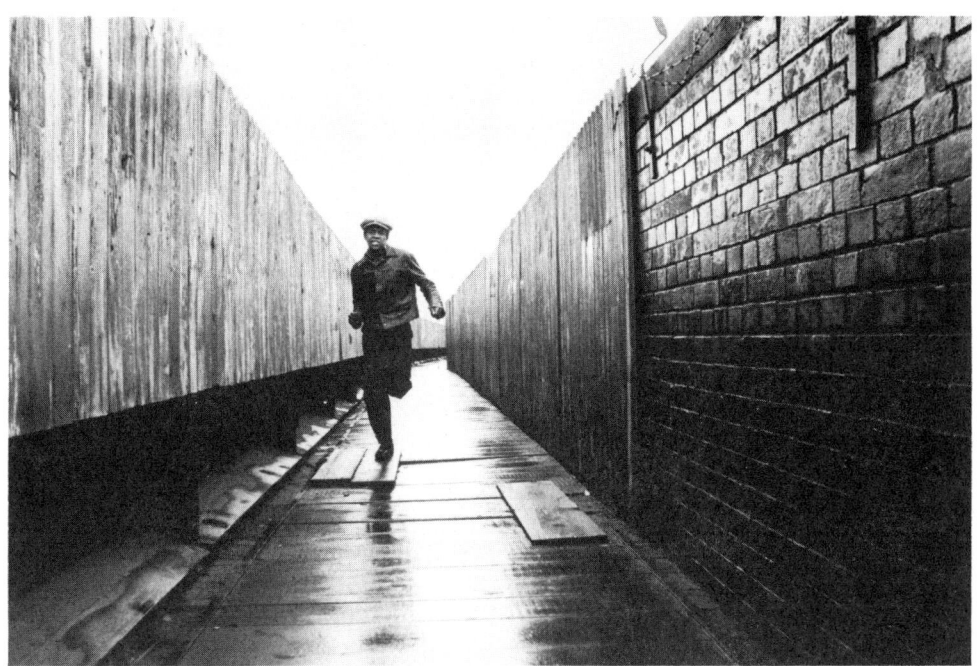

PRESSURE: Horace Ove, courtesy of: Horace Ove

of a British-born Black school-leaver's disillusionment and growing politicization as he encounters rampant racism and discrimination had a timely message which highlighted from a Black perspective—perhaps for the first time in any British film—the contradictions and impossibilities inherent in the idea of "Black British." In this respect, certain aspects of the film can be "read" as a critique of the race relations "industry," which of course has been instrumental in "professionalising" race relations, and of (British) society's failure to progress even in the light of a new generation of British-born Black people who are patently not "immigrants" in the stereotypical race-relations sense.

Identity is a central theme in *Pressure* and is most sharply articulated in the context of the boy's family. Thus, the Black family represents the site of intense intergenerational conflict, an archetypal theme in sociological race relations, with the conflict revolving around the British-born youth's precarious sense of "Britishness."

The boy's unstable identity gradually disintegrates as the story progresses; he is pulled in two ideologically opposing directions. On the one hand, his "first-generation immigrant" parents, especially the mother, try to impose a set of values and expectations which are based on an ideal notion of the complete assimilation of their British-born progeny, while an opposing set of values is represented by the boy's Caribbean-born militant brother, who constantly chides him about his lifestyle and exposes the contradictions and futility in "trying to be like the English." The boy's angst is further compounded by his encounters in the outside world, which have a traumatic impact on his whole being and lead him inevitably to a "non-English," stridently Black, identity position. Hence his politicisation through his identification with the brother's values and the concomitant rejection of his parents' view of the world. Despite the apparent radicalness of this narrative, the film's closing image of Black political protest is less progressive or "positive" than

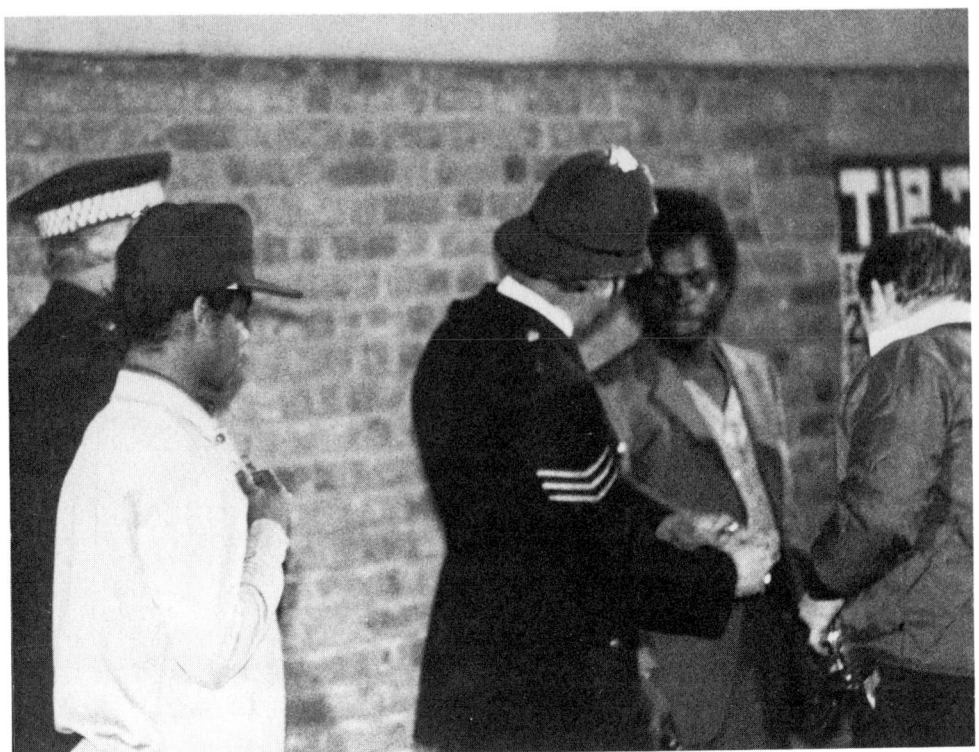

BURNING AN ILLUSION: Menelik Shabazz, courtesy of: Menelik Shabazz

it might appear, being more pessimistic in effect. But a more serious criticism is the film's representation of women, which leaves much to be desired, particularly the image of the "misguided" mother figure who is identified as the cause of the family's "failure to make it in Britain," and that of the militant leader who "seduces" the boy into the movement. These stereotypical motifs betray the film's chauvinism and, in my view, effectively undermine any possibility of a more enlightened sense of gender relationships from being developed in the narrative.

Menelik Shabazz's *Burning an Illusion* (1981), the second Black feature film funded by the British Film Institute, marked an important advance in terms of addressing questions of "race" and Black cultural politics in Black narrative fiction. It is not concerned with "race relations" as such, but focuses instead on interpersonal relationships within a Black community setting, particularly between men and women, and how these relationships change with Black consciousness and cultural politicisation. Like *Pressure*, the narrative has a linear structure and centres on the political awakening of the central character, in this case a Black woman, whose initial social conformity and political naivete gradually evolve into an active political consciousness. This political transformation is framed by the young woman's relationship with her proud-hearted boyfriend whose arrest, imprisonment, and ill treatment by the authorities propel her to "de-colonise" her mind, as a Black woman. Thus, she gradually strips herself of "bourgeois" values and identifications (e.g., the desire for conformist respectability) and begins to adopt a more strident

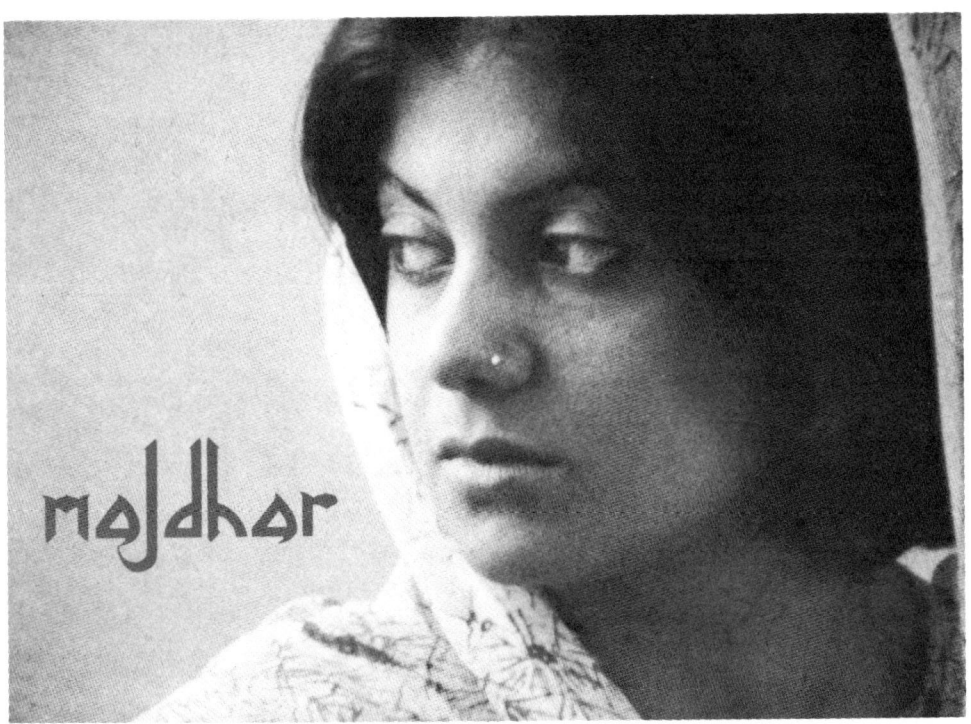

MAJDHAR: courtesy of: Retake Film and Video Collective

Black presence (e.g., her "straightened" hair becoming "locks"). In a sense, she changes her identity.

Whereas the identity crisis in *Pressure* centres largely on the dissolution of "Black British-ness," in *Burning an Illusion* it is built around the notion of Black identity being defined positively within its own terms of reference, that is, in relation to "the Black community." The question of "British-ness," therefore, does not arise as a central issue. It has no real relevance in the context of the film's representation of Black experiences. Consequently, racial victimization—i.e., the image of Blacks as "victims," a familiar motif in race-relations discourse—is not a major concern here, despite its appearance at key moments in the story. Rather, it functions as a plot device which drives the narrative along, nothing more. Indeed, the police raid on the Black club is presented as a given occurrence which needs no further development in terms of "race relations." Instead, the film uses this "moment" as a way of signalling how these kinds of racial antagonism have an impact upon relationships between Black people within "the community," especially politically. In stressing these kinds of intra-ethnic or intra-Black community concerns, *Burning an Illusion* helped to bring a more militant tone to representing Black experiences in narrative fiction. It also captured much of the mood of a new generation of British Blacks who would challenge the whole basis of British race relations by the early 1980s.

Pressure and *Burning an Illusion* are both landmark films, and they aptly reflect the major concerns of the periods in which they were made. Needless to say, the years separating them also indicate the extent to which Black independent film-

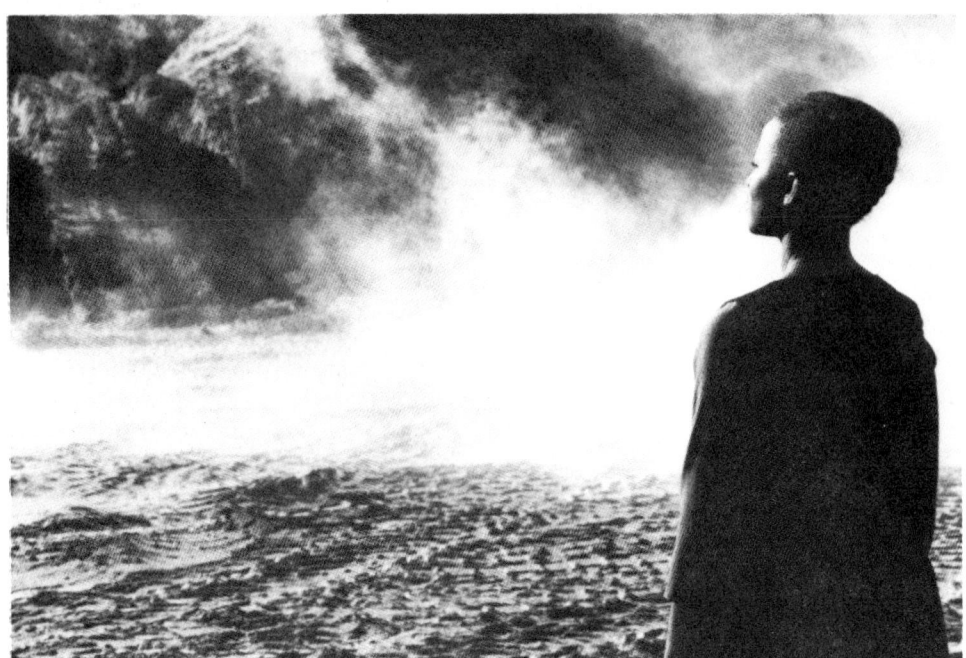

PASSION OF REMEMBRANCE: Sankofa Film/Video Production, courtesy of: Sankofa Film/Video Production

making has been marginalized in Britain, especially in terms of feature-film production. Ahmed Jamal's *Majdhar* (1984) and Horace Ove's *Playing Away* (1986) are the only other notable features that have come out of the Black independent sector in recent years, although the latter might well qualify as a "mainstream" film by virtue of its million-pounds-plus budget! *Majdhar* is especially interesting because, like the two earlier Black features, it focuses on the theme of (cultural) identity, although in an Asian context. The story concerns a young Pakistani woman who is forced to adopt a new lifestyle when she is abandoned by her unfaithful husband and left to fend for herself in Britain. Her new "independence" leads to a series of "discoveries" about the outside world, and after some anxious moments she gradually begins to adopt more "Western" (British) attitudes and lifestyles. While not having quite the same political thrust as *Burning an Illusion*, and being somewhat ambivalent about the morality of the central character's transformation, *Majdhar* is nonetheless an interesting film and, significantly, is similar in its essentially male-oriented representation of Black women's identity and politicisation.

IV

Of course none of these films really comes to grips with (Black) women's political consciousness. At best, they deploy women characters as emblematic figures whose identities are constructed ultimately through men and through (Black) male notions of politicised Black femininity. Hence the significance of Sankofa's *The Passion of Remembrance* (1986), which not only signals the most recent break with conventional race relations and multicultural representation in British-made Black films, but also takes on broad questions of gender and sexuality from a Black "feminist" perspective. The "story" is constructed around a series of dramatic moments, in which characters' personal histories intertwine with the history of political protest in ways that defy simple explanations based on race politics alone. The film makes extensive use of archival footage, which is re-processed and re-presented in the form of montages celebrating political struggle and solidarity. These documentary "moments" are framed by vignettes of Black family life, social interactions, and relationships which cut across generational differences and highlight the diversity of Black experiences. There is no homogeneous "Black community" in this construction, only "Black communities" in the explicitly plural sense.

The drama is set against the backdrop of crisis-ridden Britain in the 1980s, although it is not specifically concerned With the "British crisis." Rather, it uses this motif to develop the theme of Black people living through and (re-)defining their identities for themselves, and not in relation to the dominant. This is built around the idea of historical memory and how our sense of the past—historic moments in Black people's political struggle, for example—is brought to bear on the present. As the film's title suggests, these reverential moments of remembering are fraught with ambiguities and contradictions, in the sense that each successive generation seems to immortalize its own contributions to history and to imbue its own struggles with highly charged symbolism, which subsequent generations are compelled to live through. While acknowledging the importance of this often mythologised historical past, the film nevertheless invites us to reappraise precisely what it entails in terms of how Black people define and experience their reality, psychically as well as politically, and to consider its implications for the future. Thus, the hitherto neglected subject of Black women's role in political struggle—for example, the relationship between Black women (the mythical tea-makers) and Black men (the mythologised action figures)— becomes a crucial one which the film explores with lucid forcefulness. The result is an engaging critique of Black political culture which, more than just redressing the gender balance in Black narrative, goes a long way towards recasting Black themes and imagery in a form otherwise absent in British film and television (racial) representation.

In the broader context of British independent cinema, it has to be stressed that this kind of formal experimentation with (Black) narrative and representation could only be a main preoccupation within the grant-aided workshop sector, where political, cultural, aesthetic, and pedagogic debates are an integral part of film and video cultural practice. But it would be a mistake to therefore ignore the importance of non-workshop independents, or to evalute their contributions pejoratively in comparison, just because of their relatively mainstream orientation. The fact is, this quasi-commercial sector is not "protected" or cushioned by a structure of grants and subsidies and, therefore, it is obliged to compete in the highly competitive commercial marketplace. By definition, the nature of their practice does not allow them the "space" for formal experimentation. Nevertheless, they have made important interventions in terms of penetrating mainstream media institutions—for example, in the area of employment in the film and television industries—and in that respect they have worked towards de-marginalizing Black film and television production. Moreover, despite growing institutional support for Black film and video, cultural and professional marginalisation remains a critical problem which affects Black practitioners as a whole, irrespective of their individual creative or artistic proclivities. In other words, the whole of the Black independent film/video sector is obliged to engage in some form of institutional struggle, in order to secure greater access to otherwise limited (and rapidly diminishing) resources.

This is partly the reason why recent initiatives around Black film/video distribution and exhibition are so important, because in a very real sense these areas of film culture provide some chance of longevity for the Black independent sector as a whole. Of course there is no sense in which we can conceive Black audiences as a homogeneous entity, because in reality they are not. Therefore, Black film and video practitioners are obliged to think seriously about ways of addressing these different (Black) audiences, and about how to promote different kinds of Black and Third World films generally. It is no longer simply a matter of showing the films, but rather building into film distribution and programming strategy some form of pedagogic practice, to enable audiences to participate directly in the cultural debates around Black and Third World film cultures. Some work in this area has already begun, for example, in the screenings and distribution-related projects organised by a number of workshops and other media-related Black organisations. A number of white independent venues like regional film theatres are also beginning to make an effort to include more Black and Third World films in their programmes. But perhaps the most significant development in recent years has been the growing number of Black community-based venues across the country—such as social clubs, community centres, and cultural associations—which are becoming increasingly involved in film and television exhibition and in other media education-related activities. In some respects, this has been one of the most fertile areas of growth within the Black film/ video sector, encompassing a fairly broad constituency including both young and older-generation Black people. The emergence of these community-based venues is also interesting because it represents a potentially stable network of exhibition outlets, where the whole range of film cultural issues can be taken up, debated, and consolidated for the future.

These new developments clearly point to the emergence of a definable Black film and video sector in Britain, which encompasses not just production, but distribution, exhibition, educational work, and critical practice as well. It is this sense of growing cohesion, which has been evolving steadily since the early 1980s, that prompts one to thinking in terms of an emerging Black film culture, although we are still at an embryonic stage in this regard. Obviously the sector comprises disparate groups and practices, whose creative expressions are informed by different histories and cultural experiences. But this should not detract from the real advances which have already been made within the Black independent film and video sector, and the impact that they have had on the wider British cultural scene. And though the pervasive power of dominant representation, along with that of institutional marginalisation, has tended to impose serious constraints on Black film practice historically, e.g. by pigeonholing it in "race relations," the signs today are that these constraints are gradually being whittled away by Black cultural practitioners themselves. Moreover, Black film/video practice clearly has a cultural dynamic of its own which cannot (and should not) be reduced simply to the exegesis of oppositional practice. We therefore need to begin developing critical methods which are capable of addressing this dynamic in fairly specific terms, and with the aim of securing the important relationship between the practitioner, the critic, and the audience in a much more meaningful way.

FILM IN ANGLOPHONE AFRICA: A Brief Survey

Manthia Diawara

Feature-film production in Anglophone countries in Africa is either non-existent or just beginning. After independence, the Anglophone states, except for Nigeria and Ghana, did not attempt to integrate films as an essential element of development and/or entertainment. Most of them stopped production with the closing of the British Colonial Film Units that had supplied them with documentaries and educational films. Film specialists and amateurs alike have given many reasons as to why Anglophone Africa has not been extensively involved in film production. Some argue that it is because the British did not have an assimilationist policy toward their colonies. Unlike the French, who taught "Nos ancetres les gaulois" to Africans, the British colonialism is supposed to have been strictly business, and has never succeeded or tried the assimilation that has been linked to French colonialism.[1] Another argument pertaining to the relative poverty of Anglophone African cinema is that film is not a priority in developing countries. The Anglophone countries direct their energies, therefore, to more pressing economic problems. While they accept a few documentaries dealing with "reality," i.e. hard facts, they shun fiction, make believe and metaphysics. They are empiricists, and, according to Hannes Kamphausen, they insist "on more practical and pragmatic attitudes inherited from the former British authority."[2]

Manthia Diawara
Assistant Professor
Department of Black Studies and
Department of French
and Italian Department
University of California, Santa Barbara

Others argue further that Anglophone Africans need cinematheques and other such cultural activities to expose themselves to world-class films and whet their appetite for production. But Ola Balogun, for his part, traces the problem to the political economy of film distribution in Anglophone Africa. Taking Nigeria as a case in point, he argues that during the colonial epoch the country consumed products made in Great Britain, including films. Balogun explains that the political independence of Nigeria was not followed by an economic independence. He states that "still today, the film distribution in Nigeria is in the hands of foreign companies which dictate their will in the matter of cinema. Since distributors and exhibitors benefit more in buying, at a very low price, old American, English and Indian films, their policy has then consisted in discouraging all attempts to create a national film production."[3]

Recently, some Anglophone states have encouraged film production either by nationalizing distribution and raising subsidies from the exhibition of foreign films to finance national productions, or by funding such productions through state-sponsored agencies. In Zimbabwe, for example, the government recently set up a production and training center with the help of the Federal Republic of Germany, which was also responsible for the National Film and Television Institute (NAFTI) in Ghana and the Kenya Institute of Mass Communication (KIMC). The production center in Zimbabwe has trained filmmakers and technicians who, so far, have made newsreels, documentaries and short fiction films. In Tanzania, the Audio Visual Institute has been in existence since 1974, donated by the government of Denmark. It contains facilities for processing, printing and mixing of narrative and sound effects. The Institute provides training for filmmakers and technicians, and produces educational, publicity and documentary films. In the past years the Institute participated in international film festivals in Mogadishu (Somalia) and Ouagadougou (Burkina Faso), presenting docu-dramas on the teaching of the *Ujamaa*. In 1985, a Tanzanian co-production, *Arusi ya Mariamu* (*The Wedding of Mariamu*), directed by Nanga Yoma Ngoge and Ron Mulvihill (U.S.A.), was awarded the prize for the best short film at the Pan-African Film Festival of Ouagadougou (FESPACO). *Arusi ya Mariamu* is about the traditional science of healing and the conflict between tradition and modernity.

Like Tanzania, Kenya has just begun its interest in feature-film production. Two government branches, the Kenya Film Corporation (KFC) and The Kenya Institute of Mass Communication (KIMC), handle film activities in Kenya. The KFC deals primarily with distribution, which it has monopolized since 1972. In Kenya, as in other Anglophone countries, U.S. films dominate the market, challenged only by Indian melodramas and Kung fu movies. Since its creation, the KFC has distributed a few African films from Cameroon and Ghana, one of which, *Love Brewed . . . in the African Pot* (1980, directed by Kwaw Ansah), is the third most popular film in the country, grossing 1,022,443 Kenyan Shillings.[4] The KFC also used to distribute American films in Tanzania, Somalia, Ethiopia, Zambia and Uganda.

Other functions of the KFC involve the development of a mobile cinema system in the rural areas and video centers on the outskirts of Nairobi. According to Sharad Patel, "these films on wheels reach 500 semi-urban and rural centers a month, attracting audiences of over 40,000 every evening. And thanks to advertising, not a single one of these movie-goers pays even a cent for this entertainment."[5] Therefore, the KFC limits its film production to videotaping urban products for advertisement in rural areas, and television commercials.

The KIMC, on the other hand, has facilities in 16mm production and laboratories where filmmakers train for the Kenyan television. So far the KIMC has produced tourist-attraction films (*Waters of Mombasa*, *Passport to Adventure*, *Immashoi ol Massai*, directed by Sao Gamba), educational documentaries and other information films. In 1985, Sao Gamba directed *Kolormask*, a didactic film about a Kenyan student who returns home with a white wife. The marriage is threatened by social and cultural differences between Kenya and England. Presented at the 1987 Pan-African Film Festival, *Kolormask* was criticized for being too exotic in its emphasis on documenting African cultures. The real promise in Kenyan cinema may come from creative writers such as Ngugi Wa Thiong'o and Meja Mwangi, who are now turning to cinema, as did Ousmane Sembene in Senegal and Wole Soyinka in Nigeria, for a more direct way of communicating with their audiences. Ngugi participated in the 1986 Edinburgh Film Festival, where he presented a short video about South Africa and discussed the film course he had taught in Sweden. As for Meja Mwangi, he was listed as an assistant director in *Out of Africa* (1986), and his novel, *Carcase of Hound*, was adapted into film by Ola Balogun.

The only countries in Anglophone Africa to have gone beyond the government productions to create an independent cinema are Ghana and Nigeria. Film production continues to progress in these countries despite the lack of strong support from their governments. In Ghana, independent directors like King Ampaw and Kwaw Ansah have replaced the old documentary tradition with feature films which blend comedy and melodrama, and draw their

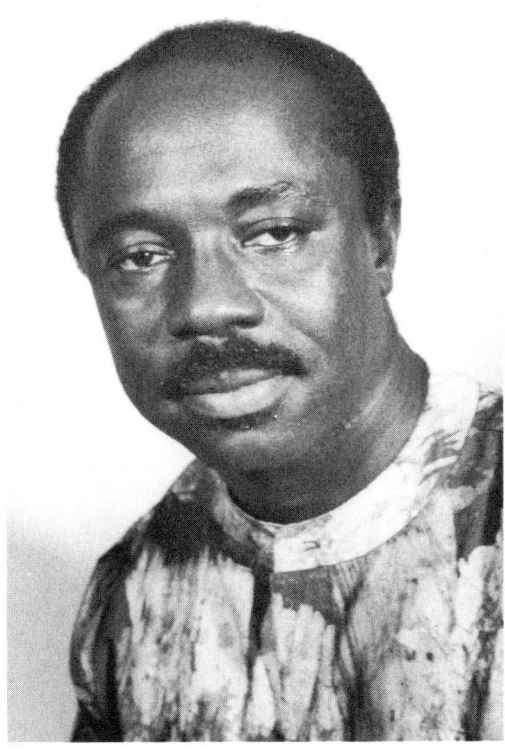

KWAW ANSAH: courtesy of: Kwaw Ansah

themes from popular culture and the meeting between Western and African civilizations. In Nigeria, a Yoruba cinema has emerged since the early '70s to become an original expression of directors like Ola Balogun and Bankole Bello, and popular Yoruba theater stars such as Chief Hubert Ogunde, Ade Folayan and Moses Olaiya Adejumo.

The government branches that handle film industry in Ghana are The Ghana Film Industry Corporation (GFIC), the Ghana Broadcasting Corporation (GBC) and The National Film and Television Institute (NAFTI). Like similar government agencies in Kenya and Tanzania, the GFIC, the GBC and the NAFTI manage the distribution, censorship, training of technicians and production of documentary and information films. The GFIC inherited the facilities of the Gold Coast Colonial Film Unit, which specialized in the documentary genre in the tradition of John Grierson. It is still possible to find in the archives of the GFIC pre-independence classics like *The Boy Kumasenu*, a film about city life, as well as post-independence Nkrumah-era classics like *Tongo Hamile*, which is a screen adaptation of Shakespeare's *Hamlet*.

The GFIC has 16mm and 35mm production equipment with laboratory facilities. With GFIC alone, Ghana is better equipped than all of the other West African states, and it is capable of turning out more than 12 features a year. Ghanaian filmmakers trained at NAFTI and abroad find their first employment at GFIC and GBC. It is in this sense that one can find the influence of GFIC's documentary style on such best-known Ghanaian directors as Sam Aryete (*No Tears for Ananse*, 1968); Egbert Adjesu (*I Told You So*, 1970); Kwate Nee-Owo (*You Hide Me*, 1971; *Struggle for Zimbabwe*, 1974; *Angela Davis*, 1976); King Ampaw (*They Call It*

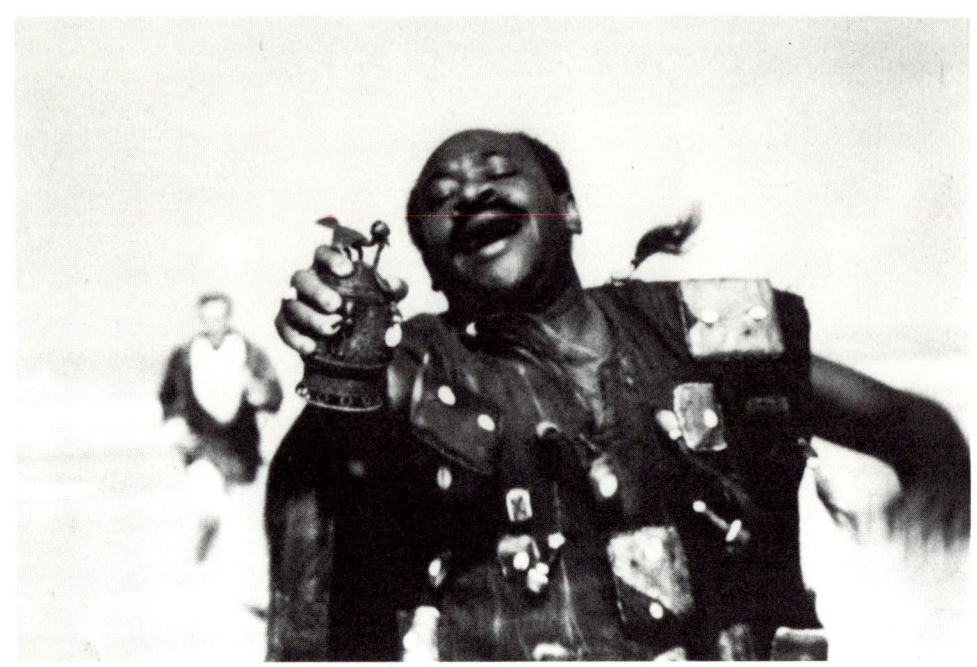

HERITAGE: Kwaw Ansah, courtesy of: Kwaw Ansah

Love, 1972; *Kukurantumi*, 1983; *Juju*, 1986); and Kwaw Ansah (*Love Brewed . . . in the African Pot*, 1980).

The GFIC manages distribution and censorship in such a manner that national and Third World films are shown in the movie theaters in Ghana. It is pushing the government, for example, to put a quota on film import and to encourage film exchange between Third World countries. It is in this vein that "Cuba and Ghana have run seasons of each other's films and the Havana festival had a retrospective of African cinema in 1986."[6] The GFIC has had to deal with video piracy, too, because the shortage of foreign currency in Ghana makes the import of films expensive. Since 1982, video centers have opened everywhere in the big cities, and the most recent films are shown on video monitors in violation of the copyright and the cinematograph laws in Ghana. More importantly, the pirated videos contribute to the economic crisis through the evasion of exhibition taxes, and the uncensored showing of pornographic films which affect the patrons negatively.[7]

Unlike the case in Kenya and Tanzania, where film production is in the hands of the government, Ghanaian cinema is not limited to the productions of GFIC, GBC and NAFTI. Ghana's best known directors, King Ampaw and Kwaw Ansah, are independent directors who produce their films by raising funds locally and internationally. Ansah's latest film, *Heritage*, for example, is funded by the Social Security Bank, the Ghana Commercial Bank, the National Investment Bank and the Cooperative Bank.[8] The relative freedom which the independent directors acquire in being their own producers enables them to make popular films that are not burdened by didactic and propagandistic precepts imposed by the government. This is not to say, however, that independent directors do not need governments and their agencies. On the contrary, both Ansah and

Ampaw use the equipment and personnel of the GFIC, and the facilities provided by such government departments as the army. Furthermore, filmmakers need the government to set quotas on film import and reduce entertainment tax for local films, so that their films can compete with foreign products.

The significance of producing independently is seen in the fact that Ansah and Ampaw choose their films on an artistic and financial basis, not on the basis that the government wants this or that type of film made. It is this artistic freedom that enables them to go beyond the documentary tradition fostered by the GFIC and to look to popular culture as a source of fictional inspiration. As Jim Pines points out, their "films draw on local culture and experience"[9] and thus ensure a box office return both in Ghana and in other African countries. The films of Ampaw and Ansah blend comedy and melodrama, ridiculing eccentric paternal figures and emphasizing the tragic clash between tradition and modernity. A look at the films reveals the contradiction between the values of the city and those of the village: they denounce acculturation and attempt to raise the consciousness of the characters in the end.

In *Love Brewed . . . in the African Pot*, for example, Ansah draws upon elements from Ghanaian cultural experience to construct a narrative with the themes of repression and class difference. The story is about a love affair between Aba, educated in a posh Cape Coast school and trained as a dressmaker, and Joe Quansah, a semi-literate auto mechanic (fitter) and son of a fisherman. Aba's father, Koffi Appiah, who is a civil servant, wants her to marry a lawyer, Bensah, instead of Joe.[10] The film thematizes repression by putting into play two of the most effective dream sequences in African cinema. The first dream shows Koffi Appiah's repressed origin return to haunt him. Ansah positions the spectator in this dream sequence by describing the fishermen's tradition as a source of pride and authenticity, which has a deeper influence on Koffi Appiah's mind than the surface appearance of Western civilization among Ghanaian elites. This silent cinematic message satisfies the unconscious expectation of African audiences, the majority of whom come from traditions similar to those of the fishermen in the film. The violence with which Koffi Appiah is punished by his unconscious serves not only to vindicate the fishermen who are humiliated by him, and with whom the spectator identifies, but also to awaken the elites like Koffi Appiah who run away from tradition and mimic the West.

The other dream sequence concerns the return of Aba's worst repressed fears in the shape of a witch. Aba's desire to marry Joe, a "fitter" beneath her class, is in violation of class differences and of her father's interdiction of such a transgression. Aba overlooks these obstacles by simplifying and dismissing her father's Westernized ideals as irrational, grotesque and superficial. On the other hand, she romanticizes the fishermen's tradition, which Joe represents, as strong, natural, music-loving and authentic. However, when the forces of class difference turn Joe against her, she is no longer able to dismiss them as irrational and grotesque. In Aba's dream, her unconscious thematizes all the obstacles into the shape of a witch, dressed in a white dress, that chases her, beats her up, changes faces, and cooks her in a pot. In her dream, Aba succumbs to a powerful monster which, while awake, she dismisses as superficial and grotesque. Ansah has been criticized for failing to construct a more "realistic" face mask for the witch.[11] What captivates the spectator, however, is less the realism of the form of the film than the content. In other words, the spectator accepts the dream because of its content, which is consistent with other rational elements that are presented in the story as obstacles to Joe marrying Aba. It is because the

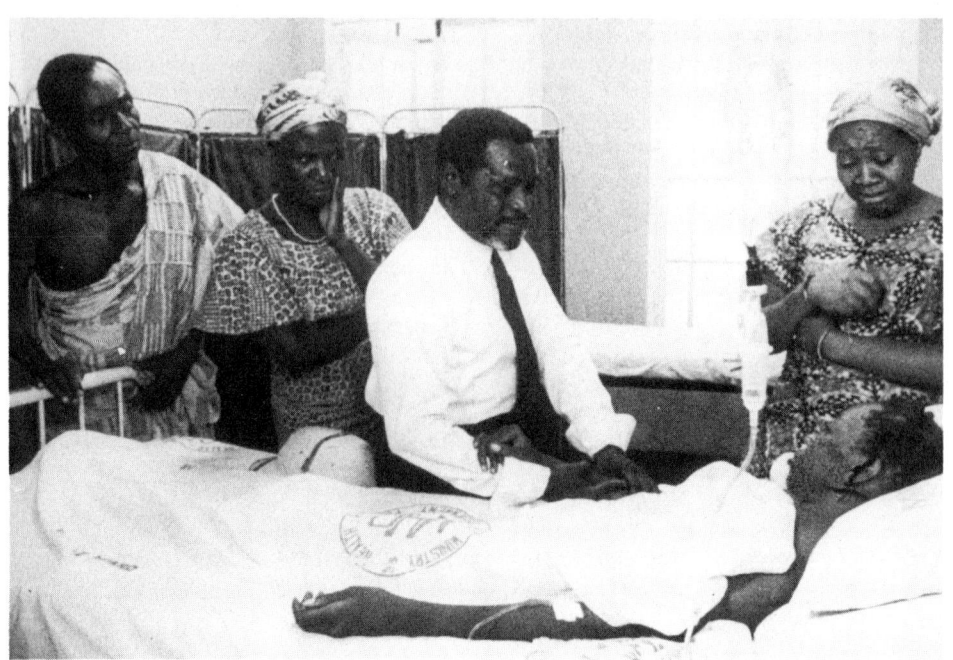

LOVE BREWED: . . . IN THE AFRICAN POT: Kwaw Ansah, courtesy of: Kwaw Ansah

representation of the dream satisfies the collective psychic need of the spectators that *Love Brewed . . . in the African Pot* beat record attendance in Kenya, Liberia and Sierra Leone, where it was screened for three months.[12] Ansah ensures the popularity of the film with African spectators by drawing from other popular experiences such as wedding ceremonies, wrestling matches and musical performances.

The government in Nigeria manages the film industry through three agencies: the Film Unit, the Nigerian Film Corporation and the National Film Distribution Company. The Film Unit, which was inherited from the colonial administration, produces educational documentaries and trains filmmakers for other departments of the government. As an office of the Federal government, it functions to satisfy the country's need for documentaries in agriculture, health, housing, etc. Between 1979 and 1983, the Film Unit produced 25 documentaries, 65 newsreels and 390 short information films. However, according to Francoise Balogun, who is the foremost authority in Nigerian film, the productions of the Film Unit do not reach a wide audience. "The Nigerian television is bombarded by foreign productions and it has no links with the Film Unit. Furthermore, there are no rules which require the theater owners to show a short documentary of the Film Unit before showing the feature film."[13]

The Nigerian Film Corporation (NFC) and the National Film Distribution Company (NFDC) are outgrowths of the 1972 Indigenization Act, "which gave exclusive monopoly for distribution and exhibition of feature films to Nigerians with the capital and business contracts."[14] The NFC was set up in 1979, but did not begin operating until 1982. According to Adamu Halilu, a filmmaker and former secretary of the NFC, its purpose was to promote production and to chart the course of the film industry complex. In view of the fact that films produced in Nigeria faced marketing difficulties, the NFC's role was to review distribution and to implement a quota system which would force theater owners to take one Nigerian film for every ten foreign films that they showed. The duties of the NFC also involved talking to merchant banks and businessmen on behalf of the filmmakers, and reviewing the entertainment tax with regard to Nigerian films.[15]

As for the NFDC, it has been in existence since 1981, replacing the American Motion Picture Export Association ten years after the Indigenization Act. Its functions include film importation, distribution and exhibition. The NFDC owns theaters around Lagos, and shows some of its films in the National Theater, which is equipped with 16mm, 35mm, and 70mm projectors. The National Theater contains two projection rooms with 676 seats each, and the main hall with 5000 seats. In 1982, 42 films were shown there, including *Orun Mooru* and *Money Power* by Ola Balogun and *Love Brewed . . . in the African Pot* by Ansah.[16]

The NFDC also imports films for other national distribution agencies such as the Nigerian Motion Picture Corporation and the West African Pictures Corporation. All these companies show Nigerian films in their theaters; however, they charge more for them in order to make the same amount of profit they make for less expensive foreign films which have already recouped their cost of production before reaching Nigeria. Nigerian filmmakers have pleaded with the government to reduce or completely eliminate the entertainment tax for local films, so that they can compete with American and Kung fu films, which flood the market. As Ola Balogun puts it, "the most that the government can do and should do is to help regulate film distribution and exhibition in such a way as would permit an individual Nigerian filmmaker to progress."[17]

The most important state participation in feature film production involves Adamu Halilu's *Shaihu Umar* (1976), which was totally financed by the government for the Nigerian entry in the 1977 FESTAC. The film, which tells the epic story of a Hausa religious leader, is based on a novel in Hausa by the first Prime Minister of Nigeria, Sir Abubakar Tafawa-Balewa. Even though *Shaihu Umar* is important because of its use of Hausa tradition and historiography, its glorification of Islam and the Hausa past, it risks letting the spectator down because of its length (2hrs- 20mns), and the repetitious long scenes.

Independent production continues to progress in Nigeria, despite the difficulties mentioned above, because of the Indigenization Act, which enables the filmmakers to distribute their films and recoup the cost of production. Since 1972, for example, Ola Balogun has become the most prolific director in Sub-Saharan Africa, producing at least one feature film a year. Balogun's films enjoy a big success in Nigeria, which lets him recoup his money each time and make new films. In 1978, he made *Black Goddess*, a film about Afro-Brazilians who returned to Nigeria

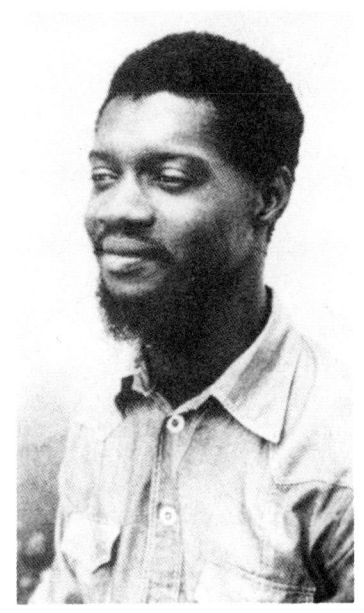

Ola Balogun: courtesy of: Ola Balogun

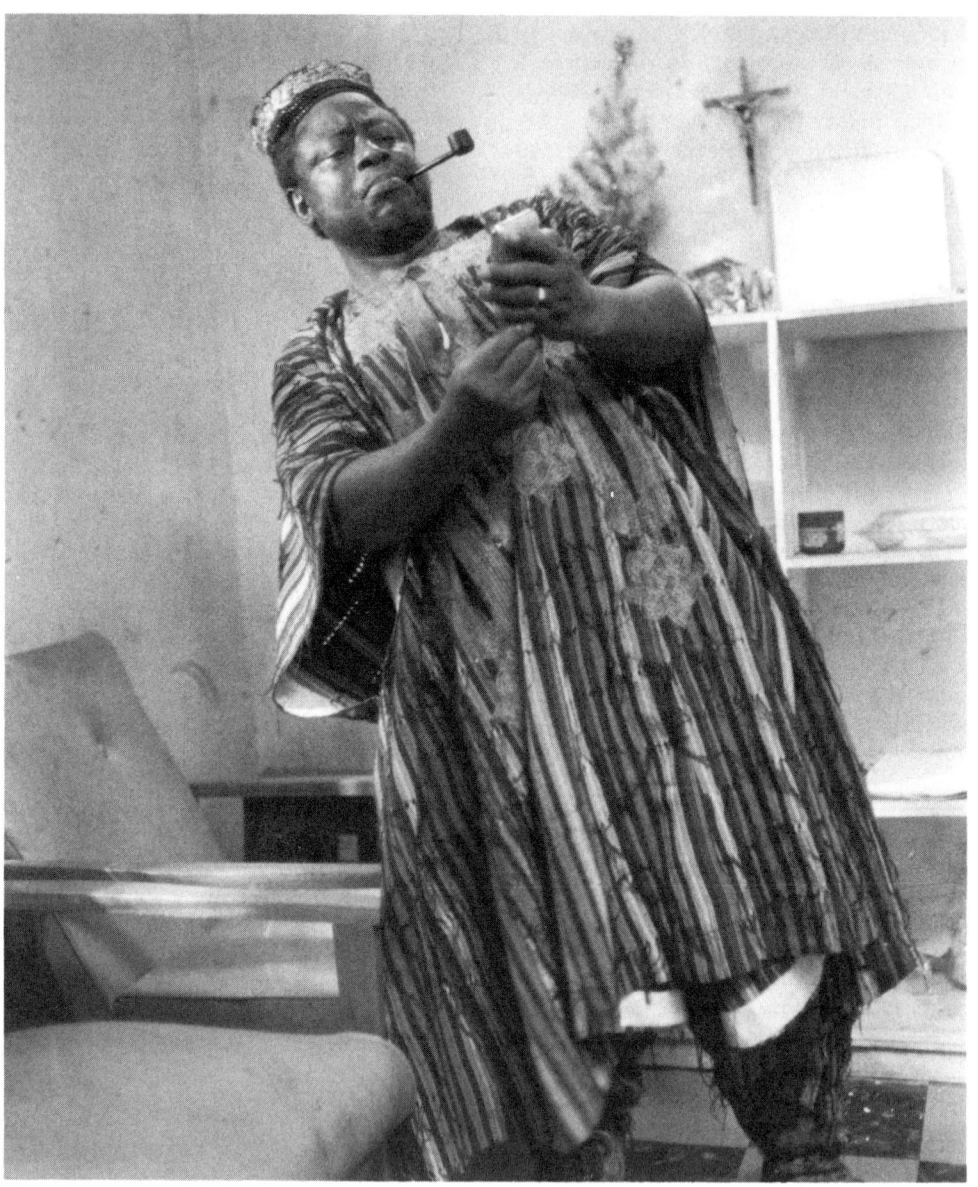

MONEY POWER: Ola Balogun, Courtesy of: Ola Balogun

after gaining freedom from slavery. It traces the roots of Babatunde, whose ancestor, Prince Oluyole, was captured in a tribal war and sent to Brazil as a slave two centuries ago. Babatunde travels from Lagos to Rio de Janeiro with the sculpture of the Goddess Yemanja which he hopes will be recognized by the part of the family that remained in Brazil. During a religious ceremony in Rio, Elisa, daughter of a priestess, reveals to Babatunde that what he is looking for is in the Bahia region. The mythico-poetic and historical aspects of *Black Goddess* are appealing to film critics. Even though the film did not meet the same success in Nigeria as the films based on popular Yoruba theater, it was internationally acclaimed, winning the award of the *Office Catholique International du Cinema*. It also won an award for the best musical score at Carthage (1980).[18] In fact, Balogun's international reputation is no longer in doubt, with such features as *Cry Freedom* (1981), a film about liberation movements and based on the novel *Carcase for Hounds* by Meja Mwangi (Kenya), and *Money Power* (1982), which have more universal themes which would appeal to audiences beyond the frontiers of Nigeria.

Eddie Ugbomah comes after Balogun with more than eight feature-films produced since 1976. Ugbomah's films are inspired by contemporary events and politics in Nigeria. His first feature, *The Rise and Fall of Dr. Oyenusi* (1977), is based on a true story about a Lagos gangster in the '70s who was arrested and executed publicly. *The Mask* (1979) shows how a fictitious Nigerian president sent a secret agent to retrieve the famous mask of Queen Adesua of Benin, which was stolen by British colonizers and put in a London museum. The film, starring Ugbomah himself, uses the Manichean aesthetics of the James Bond films, thematizing the Nigerian hero as super clever, and the British police as stupid. T*he Death of a Black President* (1983) is based on the events leading to the assassination of General Murtala Mohamed, who was head of state of Nigeria between 1975 and 1976.

More importantly, the Indigenization Act has attracted the stars of popular Yoruba theater to film. In 1976, Ola Balogun made *Ajani Ogun* with Ade "Love" Folayan, who is a star in the Yoruba popular theater. The film tells the story of a young man who has to fight an evil rich man to get his fiance and his inheritance back. Long screen times are devoted to Ade Love in the title role, as he sings long romantic songs, or fights his opponents. Balogun directed the film with the help of Duro Lapido, who had a long experience directing his own plays for Nigerian television. The success of *Ajani Ogun* and the public's request for a sequel was such that Balogun and Ade Love teamed up again in 1977 to film *Ija Ominira*, a popular story about a tyrannic king who was chased out of his kingdom. *Ija Ominira* is the first Nigerian film to have recouped its cost of production within one year.[19]

The success of *Ajani Ogun* and *Ija Ominira* at the box office led other popular figures of the Yoruba theater, such as Chief Hubert Ogunde and Moses Olaiya Adejumo (alias Baba Sala), to seek out Balogun to adapt their plays to film. In 1979, Balogun and Chief Hubert Ogunde produced *Aiye*, based on a play written by Ogunde. *Aiye* is a story about a struggle between a traditional medicine man and an evil magician. The film is full of special effects which produce the sense of magic. The popularity of *Aiye* was also assured by the presence in the film of Chief Ogunde, whose name could bring loyal admirers of his theater to the movies. In 1982, another pioneer of Yoruba theater, Baba Sala produced *Orun Mooru* with Balogun. Presented to the Pan-African Film Festival of Ouagadougou in 1987, *Orun Mooru* was one of the most popular films for the spectators in Burkina Faso. Baba Sala plays Lamidi, the hero in the film, who decides to commit suicide after having been robbed by swindlers. As Limidi undertakes his journey to the kingdom of the Dead, he realizes that Death, Iku, is not ready for him. Iku sends him, therefore, to Ayo, the spirit of Joy. Ayo gives Lamidi two eggs without telling him that the first one contains wealth and the second death. Ayo sends Lamidi back to earth, advising him to break the first egg immediately upon his return home, and the second egg fifty years later. Following Ayo's recommendation, Lamidi breaks the first egg and becomes instantly wealthy. Led by greed, he thinks that he will get even richer by breaking the second egg. Yet, as Limidi breaks it open, he finds himself confronted with Death.[20]

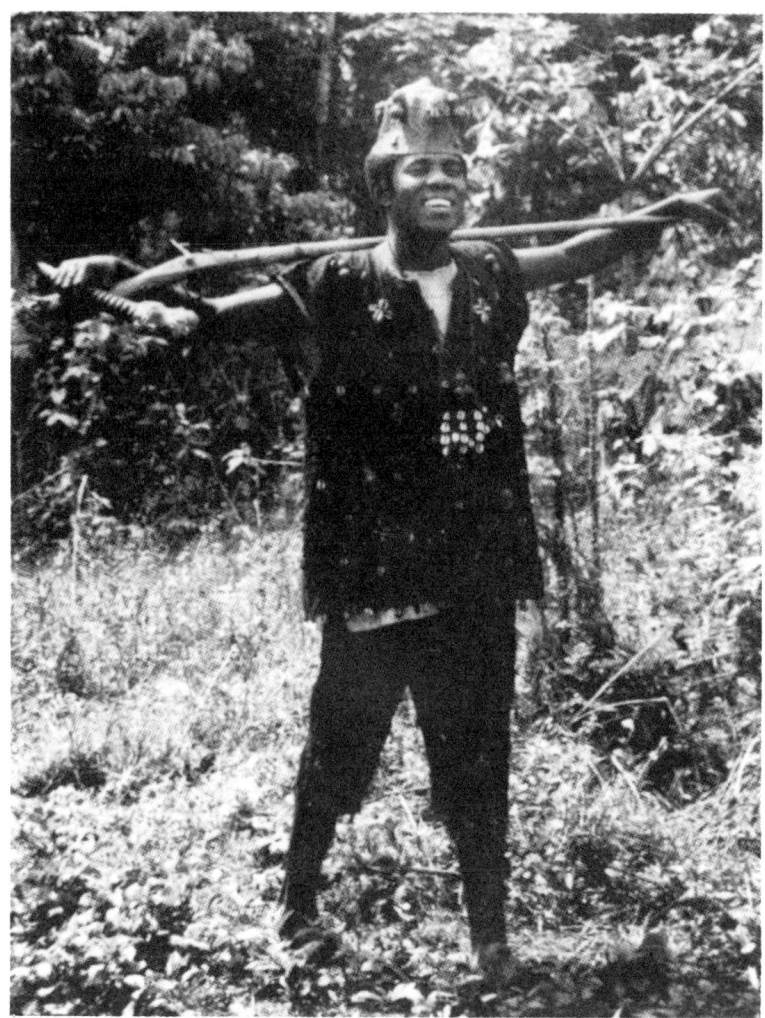

AJANI OGUN: courtesy of: Ola Balogun

Other stars of popular theater have come to cinema as a result of the commercial success of *Ajani Ogun*, *Ija Ominira* and *Orun Mooru*. In 1982, Akinwuni Isola teemed with Bankole Bello, who assisted Balogun in the production of *Ajani Ogun*, to produce *Efunsetan Aniwura*. Furthermore, Baba Sala, Ade Love and Chief Ogunde have left Balogun to fly on their own wing as producers, directors and actors of their own films. They believe that they owe their popularity at the movies less to the cinematic form that Balogun was giving to their films, and more to their own performances as stars and the illusion of reality and magic provided by film.

After this brief survey of Yoruba theater on film, what kind of evaluation can one make of it? For her part, Francoise Balogun believes that Yoruba cinema is limited to Yoruba audiences because it stresses the inside aspects of Yoruba tradition, instead of the universal aspects. "Outside of the Yoruba country, the Yoruba cinema constitute an exotic curiosity instead of an artistic expression."[21] She states also that Ola Balogun, her husband, is tired of directing "these fairy-tales" for Yoruba theater companies, and more inclined to direct films that communicate with the public at a deeper and more intellectual level.[22]

Other critics believe, on the contrary, that the future of Nigerian cinema is in Yoruba popular theater. The question becomes, then, how to operate within the social conditions of cinema and popular theater in Nigeria, and create great works of art. In the words of Luky Isawode, "Today, there are countless number of actors, dramatists, playwrights, singers, martial artists, etc., in this country. What the Indians and Chinese did, Nigerians can also do."[23]

Wole Soyinka also thinks that the Yoruba popular theater can provide Nigeria with a new art form, as well as an economically viable industry for the producers and the businessmen. The stars of popular theater have, for years of production of their plays, already shaped the taste of audiences in Nigeria. The new Yoruba cinema can make this audience its own by carefully appropriating the elements of popular theater (stars, magic, dance and music) that appeal to the spectators, and mixing them with that which cinema offers (photography, illusion of reality and magic produced by editing and putting together images, and close-ups). For Soyinka, what filmmakers need in Nigeria is an "inter-mutual interrelation" between theater and cinema, keeping in mind all the time that the two media are not exactly the same.[24]

Soyinka believes that the Yoruba cinema is economically viable because it does not resort to the aesthetic precepts which are molded by Western cinema, and which are expensive to produce in an African film. The least expensive cameras, 16mm and super 8mm, can be used in the production of Yoruba cinema without a loss of quality. Because the Yoruba theater comes to cinema already equipped with its own actors, costumes, stories and props, all the filmmaker has to do is to put the theater in a cinematic time. It is in this sense that Soyinka states his preference for cinema verite as a model for Yoruba cinema. This cinema is not only relevant to the social conditions of Nigeria because it reflects stories and spectacles based on everyday life and on the collective myths, but it also provides an aesthetic and economic alternative to the Western superproduction. For Soyinka, the Yoruba cinema can manipulate the technology provided by film to evolve a new art form for the masses, as opposed to an elitist art form open only to the intellectual.[25]

Soyinka's interest in the interrelation between theater and film is not, however, limited to these written statements. In 1971, Ossie Davis adapted his play *Kongi's Harvest* on film in which the role of Kongi, a totalitarian leader, was played by Soyinka himself. (The Nobel Prize-winning playwright has since denounced the film version of *Kongi's Harvest* as unfaithful to the script he wrote for the screen adaptation.[26]) In 1984, Soyinka directed his first feature film, *Blues for a Prodigal*.

Considering the success of Yoruba cinema in Nigeria, and the fact that the best Yoruba films like *Orun Mooru* are also popular in other African countries, it may be that filmmakers in other parts of Africa should seek a more popular form of cinema by looking at existing popular spectacles like theater, wrestling matches, song and dance. Both Nigerian and Ghanaian cinemas can learn from the mistakes and innovations of the Francophone cinema which preceded them, and which is world famous, with such directors as Ousmane Sembene and Souleymane Cisse. The movement toward popular culture constitutes a step toward giving African cinema its own identity.

It is obvious from this survey that there are enough resources in Anglophone Africa to enable the emergence of a regional and international film industry. Since the

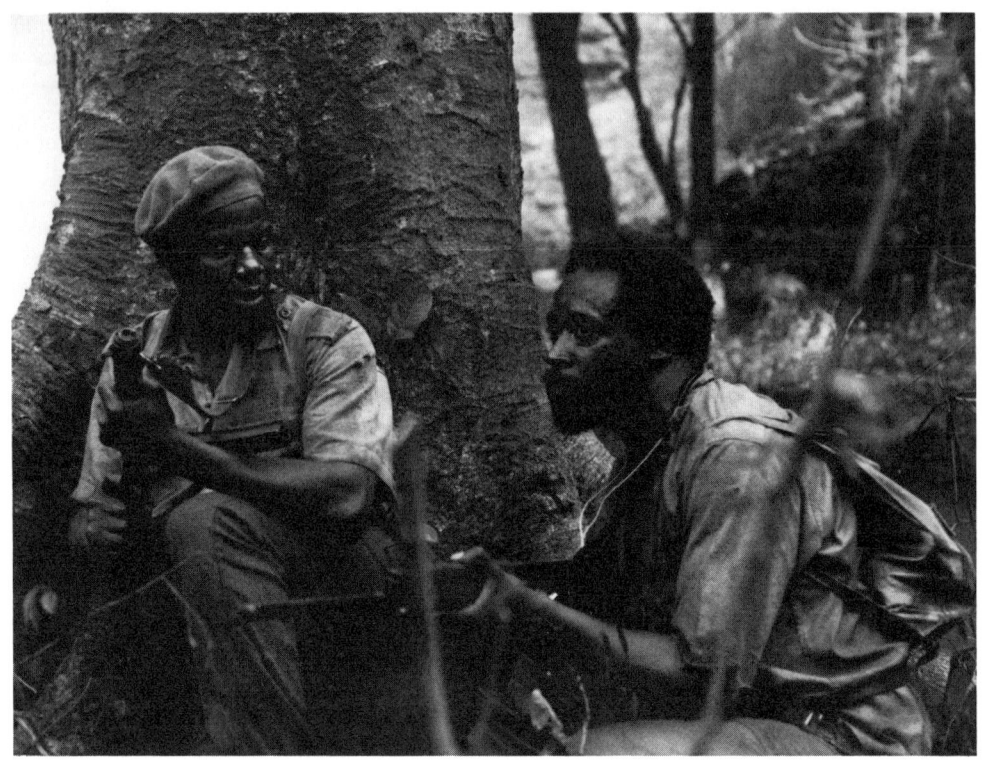

CRY FREEDOM: Ola Balogun, courtesy of: Ola Balogun

early '70s, film distribution has been nationalized in such countries as Tanzania, Kenya, Nigeria, Ghana and Ethiopia. In Nigeria, the Indigenization Act has enabled private Nigerians with the business contracts to take control of film distribution and exhibition. Not only does this create new jobs for Nigerians, but it also stimulates the economy because the revenues from distribution and exhibition remain in the country, instead of being evacuated to banks in London, Bombay or New York, which was the case when foreigners controlled the industry. A regional film distribution can also come from the nationalization of the industry. The cost of foreign films can be reduced by acquiring films through a cooperative constituted by different countries in a region. It was in this sense that Kenya used to distribute films in the '70s to Zambia, Ethiopia and Uganda. Such a regional distribution network has been in existence in Francophone Africa since 1973, even though it has yet to fight foreign distributors for the control of the market.

Distribution is also the key to national film production. Because of import quotas, France and West Germany, Europe's two most important film producers, have survived the bombardment of their film market by the U.S. Motion Picture Export Association of America (MPEAA). Similarly, a quota on the import of foreign films in Anglophone Africa can liberate more screen space for African and Third World films. For example, audiences in Anglophone Africa should be given the opportunity to see the independent Afro-American and Black British cinemas. Like France and West Germany, Anglophone countries in Africa can also raise taxes on the distribution of foreign films to subsidize national film production. At the same time, the governments can lower entertainment taxes for national films to make it easier for them to compete with the imported films.

Like film distribution, film production can also be regionalized in Anglophone Africa. So far, the coproductions take place between Africa and the West. The landscape and the people in Africa are often used as background for stories about Westerners: *King Solomon's Mines* shot in Zimbabwe, *Out of Africa* in Kenya, *Dogs of War* in Ghana, etc. With the number of filmmakers available in Africa today, it is ironic that some Anglophone African countries call upon Westerners to direct documentaries and educational films intended for Africans. Coproductions are desirable, but, if possible, they should be between African nations. There are many reasons why I assert this principle. First, by using Africans, the producers will spend less. Second, the film, by its double or triple nationality, increases the chances that it will recoup its cost among an African audience. Coproduction among Africans may also put to full use the equipment in such countries as Ghana, Kenya and Zimbabwe, where all the facilities of production exist, but feature films are rare. Most importantly, aesthetically films run far less risk of misinterpreting African cultures and reifying African people when made by African directors. Ghana has opened the way for such coproductions on the African level. In 1980, Ola Balogun shot *Cry Freedom* in Ghana with the cooperation of NAFTI. More recently John Akomfrah of the Black Audio Film Collective and director of *Handsworth Songs* (Winner of the first Paul Robeson Prize at FESPACO) has turned to Ghana for the location as well as subject of his second film. Haile Gerima, too, is looking to Ghana for a possible location for his next film.

REFERENCES

1. Ferid Boughedir in *Afrique Noire: Quel Cinema?* Paris: Actes du Colloque Universite de Paris X, Nanterre (Dec. 1981), p. 33.
2. Hannes Kamphausen, "Cinema in Africa: A Survey," in *Cineaste* (Vol. 5, No. 3), p. 31.
3. Ola Balogun, "Les trois longs metrages nigerians," *Afrique Litteraire et Artistique*, No. 124 (Special issues: "Les Cinemas Africains en 1972," 1972), p. 252.
4. Paul Lazarus, "Film Production in Kenya." Unpublished report to ICDC and KFC. (May, 1983).
5. Sharad Patel, "The Communication Gap." Unpublished paper presented to the Kenya Film Week. (Dec. 1986).
6. Janice Turner and Jai Kumar, "Shooting it Out With Rambo," *South*, (Nov. 1977), p. 93.
7. "Video Piracy in Ghana," *West Africa*, No. 3463 (Jan. 2, 1984), p. 22.
8. Nanabanyin Dadson, "The Bad Old Days," *West Africa*, No. 3655. (Aug. 31, 1987) p. 1694.
9. Janice Turner and Jai Kumar, p. 93.
10. Francoise Pfaff, *Twenty-Five Black African Filmmakers*. Westport, Conn.: Greenwood Press, 1988.
11. *Ibid*.
12. *Ibid*.
13. Francoise Balogun, *Le Cinema au Nigeria*. Paris: Editions OCIC/L'Harmatan, 1983. p. 20.
14. Manthia Diawara, *"African Cinema: The Background and the Economic Context of Production."* Unpublished dissertation, Bloomington: Indiana University (1985), p. 190.
15. Saddik Balewo, "Nigerian Film Industry," *West Africa*, No. 3513 (Dec. 1984), p. 2584.
16. Francoise Balogun, p. 25.
17. Richard Ikiebe, "Nigerian Film Industry Gets More World Attention, " *Daily Times* (May 24, 1980), p. 7.
18. Francoise Balogun, p. 66.
19. *Ibid*., p. 64.
20. Francoise Pfaff, *Twenty-Five Black African Filmmakers*.
21. Francoise Balogun, p. 87.
22. *Ibid*., p. 67.
23. "Film-making in Nigeria: Problems Inherent," *The Nigerian Standard* (Mar. 13, 1985), p. 3.
24. "Theatre and the Emergence of Nigerian Film Industry," in *The Development of the Film Industry in Nigeria*. Alfred E. Opubor and Onuora E. Nwuneli, editors. Lagos: Third Press International Division, 1979, pp. 102–103.
25. *Ibid*., p. 101.
26. *Ibid*., p. 97.

DIASPORA CULTURE AND THE DIALOGIC IMAGINATION:

The Aesthetics of Black Independent Film in Britain

Kobena Mercer

> Our imaginations processed reality and dream, like maniacal editors turned loose in some frantic film cutting room . . . we were dream serious in our efforts.
>
> Ralph Ellison[1]

The question of aesthetics arises today as a crucial issue for black filmmaking practices in Britain for two important reasons. First, significant changes in the material conditions of black politics since the early '80s have enabled a creative and prolific upsurge in black filmmaking activity in recent years. The emergence of a new generation of cinematic activists—Ceddo, Sankofa, Retake, Black Audio Film Collective —symbolises a new threshold of cultural struggle in the domain of black cinema and image-making. Their work deepens and extends the narrative and documentary frameworks for black filmmaking established by Horace Ove, Lionel Ngakane, Menelik Shabazz and others in the 1960s and '70s. And the emergence of a new "experimental" approach has also widened the parameters of black film practice, bringing a new quality of diversity to black filmmaking.

Until now, black film in Britain has emphasised the radical content of its political message over the politics of representation inherent in the medium. Certain aesthetic qualities generated by self-consciously cinematic strategies at work in new forms of black filmmaking today indicate significant shifts and critical differences in attitude to the means of representation. In this context it becomes necessary to think through the political implications of choices and decisions made at the level of film-form. If such shifts and changes within black filmmaking may be momentarily grasped as an accentuation of the expressive over the referential, or as an emphasis on the complexity rather than the homogeneity of the black experience in Britain, what is at issue is not a categorical "break" with the past but the embryonic articulation of something "new" that does not fit a pre-given category.

Second, insofar as aesthetics concerns the conceptual criteria for evaluating artistic and cultural practices, it now becomes necessary to reflect more rigorously on the role of critics and criticism. This need arises with urgency not simply because the increase in quantity at the point of production necessitates clarification of qualitative distinctions at the point of reception, but more importantly because of the bewildering range of conflicting responses provoked by new work such as *Handsworth Songs* (Black Audio Film Collective, 1986) and *The Passion of Remembrance* (Sankofa, 1986).

I would like to be able to use a word like "modernist" to describe the "shock of the

---

Kobena Mercer
Previously a Lecturer at the Centre for Carribean Studies, University of London, Goldsmiths' College, now with the British Film Institute

new" here, as responses among audiences, critics and institutions have ranged from hostile impatience to the awarding of prestigious prizes. It is precisely this dissensus that indicates something important is going on! It would be useful to note some of the terms of dissensus to grasp what is at issue. White audiences and critics have commented on the "influence" of Euro-American avant-garde cinema and film theory, which is not in itself a criticism, but nevertheless suggests an underlying anxiety to pin down and categorise a practice that upsets and disrupts fixed expectations and normative assumptions about what "black" films should look like.[2] Black audiences and critics have been similarly bemused by the originality of a practice that explicitly draws on a dual inheritance from both Third World and First World cultures, but it is interesting to note that the most vociferous critiques here concern a dispute over the political content of the films.

In particular, I want to highlight the brief debate initiated by Salman Rushdie's singularly unconstructive critique of *Handsworth Songs*, as it implicitly reveals a crisis of criticism for black cultural politics.[3] Rushdie's disdainful and dismissive response—"There's more to life in Handsworth than race riots [sic] and police brutality"—betrays a closed mind which assumes, as Stuart Hall pointed out in reply, that *"his* [Rushdie's] songs are not only different but better."* What makes Rushdie's position all the more worrying is not that the conservative literary-humanist criteria he adopts are so at odds with the open-ended textual strategies performed in his own work, but that he uses his literary "authority" to delegitimate the film's discourse and disqualify its right to speak.

As with the unfavorable review in *Race Today*[4], Rushdie enacts an appallingly authoritarian practice of "interpretation" which assumes a priori that one version of reality, his political analysis of Handsworth, has more validity, legitimacy and authority than another, the version articulated by the film. What is at stake here is the fact that there is no shared framework for a viable practice of black cultural criticism, a fact both acknowledged and disavowed by Darcus Howe's defense of Rushdie's polemic which claimed that it "[lay] the foundations of a critical tradition." To argue that a few columns of newsprint "lay the foundations" for black film criticism is to recognise that such a "tradition" does not yet exist, which itself could be read as an indictment of the kind of legitimating authority Howe arrogates to himself as "an activist in the black movement for over 20 years, organising political, cultural and artistic thrusts . . . from our black communities."

At one level, the lack of an ongoing discourse of radical black film criticism is one unhappy legacy of the marginalisation and underdevelopment of black filmmaking in Britain. This must be understood as a consequence of material conditions. Previously we had to wait so long to see a black-made film that we didn't really "criticise"; there wasn't enough space to "theorise" aesthetics; we were simply "thankful" the films got made in the first place. Moreover, we encounter a double absence here, as the "professionalisation" of critical film theory in journals like *Screen* in the '70s effectively "screened-out" black and Third World film practices, confining itself to a narrowly Euro-centric canon. At this critical conjuncture we cannot afford to merely "celebrate" the achievements of black filmmakers or act as "cheerleaders" for the so-called "ethnic arts." As Stuart Hall remarks on black cultural production generally, "we have come out of the age of innocence [which] says, as it were, 'It's good if it's there'," and are now entering the next phase in which "we actually begin to recognise the extraordinary complexity of ethnic and cultural differences."[5]

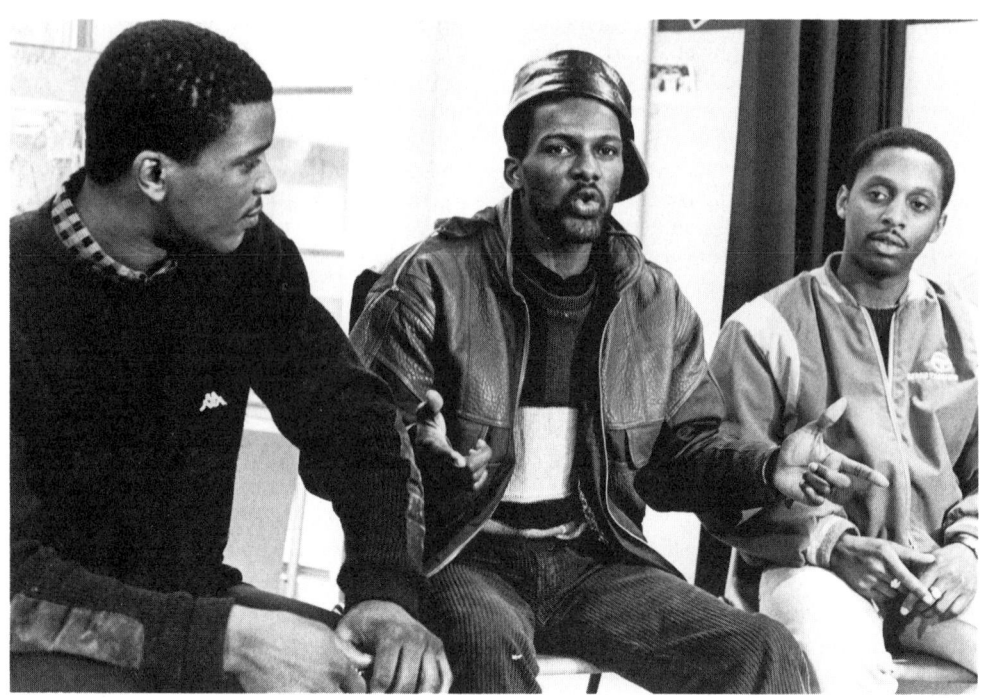

THE PEOPLE'S ACCOUNT: Ceddo Film Video Workship, Courtesy of: Ceddo Film Video Workshop

In the thick of this difficult phase of transition, my concern is to explore whether a more adequate model of criticism might not be derived from the critical practice performed in the films themselves. To the extent that what is at issue is not a struggle between one person and another but between different ways of thinking and talking about black filmmaking, a more useful and viable criterion for criticism comes from the concept of "interruption," which "seeks not to impose a language of its own [as does the practice of 'interpretation'] but to enter critically into existing configurations [of discourse] to re-open the closed structures into which they have ossified."[6]

To articulate the past historically does not mean to recognise it "the way it really was." It means to seize hold of a memory as it flashes up at a moment of danger ... Only that historian will have the gift of fanning the spark of hope in the past who is firmly convinced that *even the dead* will not be safe from the enemy if he wins.

Walter Benjamin[7]

A cursory survey of the work of black filmmakers in Britain will reveal the preponderance of a "realist" aesthetic in films made within both documentary and narrative genres. This insistent emphasis on the real must be understood as the prevailing mode in which independent black film has performed a critical function in providing a counter-discourse against those versions of reality produced by dominant voices and discourses in British film and media. Thus, the substantive concern with the politicising experience of black youth in films such as *Pressure* (dir. Horace Ove, 1974) and *Step Forward Youth* (dir. Menelik Shabazz, 1977) demonstrates a counter-reply to the criminalising stereotypes generated and amplified by media-led moral panics in the '70s.[8] Similarly, *Blacks Britannica* (1979)—although not a black British film, it is read, used and circulated as such—"gives voice" to those excluded and silenced by the discourse of media racism. This oral testimony combines with the political analysis advanced by the activists/ intellectuals featured in the film to present an alternative "definition of the situation." And as *Struggles for the Black Community* (dir. Colin Prescod, 1983) shows, the historical emphasis in this counter-discourse is an overdetermined necessity to counteract the *de*historicising logic of racist ideology.

There is significant continuity at the level of thematic concern with the politics of racism in new documentaries such as *Handsworth Songs* (dir. John Akomfrah, 1986) and *Territories* (dir. Isaac Julien, 1984). Yet important differences in the articulation of a counter-discourse on the real reveal distinct approaches to the politics of representation.

The "reality-effect" produced by realist methods depends on the operation of four characteristic values—transparency, immediacy, authority and authenticity—which are in fact aesthetic values central to the dominant film and media culture itself. By adopting a "neutral" or instrumental relation to the means of representation, this mode of black film practice seeks to redefine referential realities of race through the same codes and forms as the prevailing film language whose discourse of racism it aims to contest. Clearly we need to clarify the contradictions involved in this paradox.

By presenting themselves as transparent "windows on the world" of racism and resistance, such films emphasise the urgency, immediacy and "nowness" of their message. In the case of the "campaigning" documentary, such as *The People's Account* (dir. Milton Bryan, 1986), this is a contextual necessity, as such films perform a critical function by providing an alternative version of events so as to inform, agitate and mobilise action. However, such communicative efficacy in providing counter-information exhausts itself once the political terrain changes. Further, although it is always necessary to document and validate the authority of experience ("who feels it, knows it"), the selection of *who* is given the right to speak may also exclude others: the voices and viewpoints of black women, for example, are notable by their absence from films such as *Blacks Britannica*. Finally, the issue of authenticity, the aspiration to be "true to life" in narrative drama especially, is deeply problematic, as a given "type" of black person or experience is made to "speak for" black people as a whole. Not only does this reduce the diversity of black opinions and experiences to a single perspective assumed to be "typical," it may reinforce the tokenistic idea that a single film can be regarded as "representative" of every black person's perception of reality.

In short, black film practices which incorporate these filmic values are committed to a mimetic conception of representation which assumes that reality has an objective existence "out there," and that the process of representation simply aims to correspond to or "reflect" it. Certain limitations inherent in this conception become apparent once we contrast it to the semiotic concept of signification at work in new modes of black film discourse. My aim is not to polarise different approaches in black filmmaking, but to argue that this latter mode offers new perspectives on the real-politics of race by entering into a struggle with the means of representation itself. Foregrounding an awareness of the decisions and choices made in the selection and combination of signifying elements in sound and image, these new films are conscious of the fact that the reality-effect is constructed by the formal tendency to regulate, fix, contain and impose

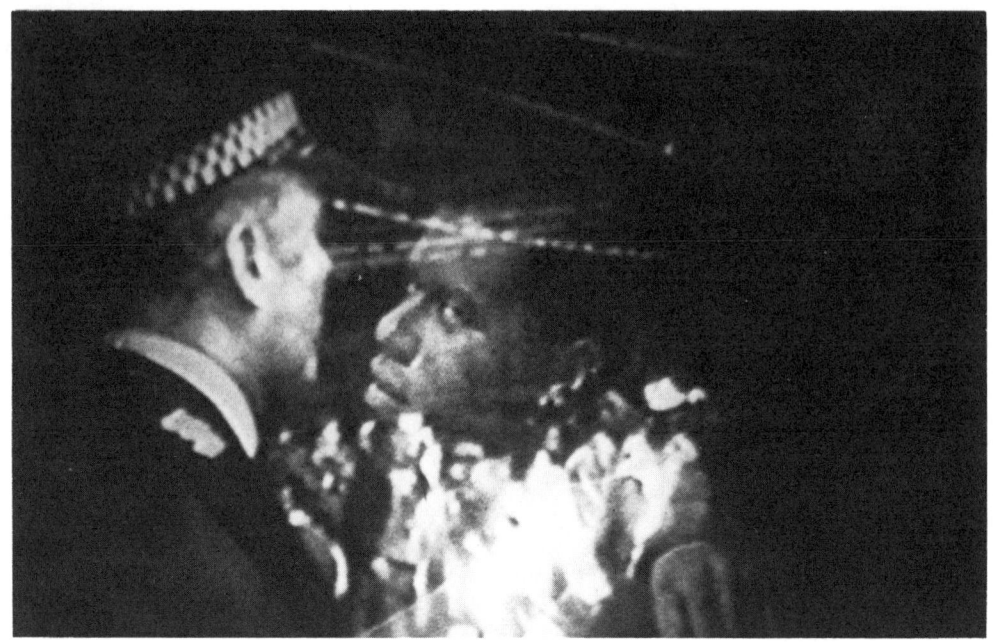

TERRITORIES: Sankofa Film/Video Production, Courtesy of: Saankofa Film/Video Production

closure on the chain of signification. By intervening at the level of cinematic codes of communication, they interrupt the ideological purpose of naturalistic illusion and perform a critical function by liberating the imaginative and expressive dimension of the filmic signifier as a material reality in its own right.

Territories is not "about" Notting Hill Carnival[9] so much as it documents the problems of trying to "represent" the complex multifaceted aesthetic and political meanings of this phenomenon of diaspora culture. Its fragmentary collage of archival and original material interrupts the transparency necessary for an "objective" account to achieve a quality of *critical reverie*. By this I mean that the openness of the film text hollows out a cognitive and affective space for critical reflection on the polyvocal dimension of Carnival—an event/process in which social boundaries and hierarchical power relations are momentarily dissolved and upended. So, rather than passively "reflect" this (which risks neutralising the subversive potential of Carnival), the text enacts or embodies the critical spirit of Carnival with "the sense of the gay relativity of prevailing truth and authority" (Bakhtin) that itself "carnivalises" codes and conventions such as space-time continuity in editing. In this way the film destabilises fixed boundaries, precisely what happened in Carnival 1976 when black youth massively reveled in the pleasure of political resistance to the policing of black culture where the state attempted to literally impose closure and containment.

Carnival breaks down barriers between active performer and passive audience. *Territories* does something similar by emphasising its performance and reflexive mode of address to enlist the participation of the spectator. Discontinuous gaps between sound and image-tracks create a rhythmic homology between the deconstructive aesthetic of dub-versioning—which "distances" and lays bare the musical anatomy of the original song through skillful re-editing which sculpts out aural space for the DJ's talk-over[10]—and the jump-cut montage principle of the film.

Its phatic mode of enunciation, highlighted by images which show two women examining footage on an editing machine, also questions the univocal captioning role of the voice-over within the documentary genre. The choral refrain—"we are struggling to tell a story"—underlines the fact that its story does not arrive at a point of closure, and this deferral of any authoritative resolution to the issues it raises implies that the spectator shares active responsibility for making semantic connections between the multiaccentuated perspectives of the image-flow. This is important because by pluralising the denotative value of given signs such as the Union Jack flag, the surplus of connotations engendered by multiple superimposition of imagery does not lead to the "infinite regression" of formalism. Of the many readings the film allows, I feel it can be said that it's a film about "self-image" because the ambivalence of its images—such as the two men entwined in an intimate embrace—is directional: its multiaccentuality is strategically anchored to raise questions about the dialectics of race, class and, especially, gender and sexuality as they cut across the public/private division in which social identities are constructed in the first place.

Handsworth Songs engages similar carnivalising strategies at the level of montage and dissonant reverberation between sound and image. The juxtaposition of actuality footage of civil disorder, on the one hand, and images drawn from "official" archive sources and "family-album" photographs, on the other, interrupts the amnesia of media-representations of the 1985 conflict in Birmingham and London. Instead of "nowness," the film reaches for historical depth, creating a space of critical reverie which counteracts the active ideological forgetting of England's colonial past in media discourses on Handsworth to articulate an alternative "archeological" account.

A female narrator tells of a journalist pestering a black woman on Lozell's Road for a news story: in the poetry of resistance, she replies, "There are no stories in the riots, only the ghosts of other stories." This reflexive comment on the intertextual logic of the film marks out its struggle to excavate and reclaim a creole counter-memory of black struggle, itself always repressed, erased and made invisible in the dominant "popular memory" of British film and media discourse. Against divisive binary oppositions between Asian/Afro-Caribbean and between first and third generations, the interweaving of the past-in-the-present through oral testimony and poetic re-encoding of archive imagery seeks to recover a "sense of intimacy"; the film itself moves to "seize hold of a memory as it flashes up at a moment of danger." It talks back to the disparaging view of our foreparents as "naive" and "innocent" by invoking the dreams and desires that motivated migrations from the Caribbean. In this way it "rescues the dead" from that amnesia and collective forgetfulness that haunt the English collective consciousness whenever it thinks of its crisis-ridden "race-relations."

History is not depicted in a linear novelistic narrative —which would imply that our stories of struggle are "over." Rather, the presence of the past in the absences of popular memory is invoked through multiple chains of association. Retinted images of chains in an iron foundry, overlaid by the eerie intonation of an English working-men's song, powerfully evoke not only the connection with the chains of slavery that made the industrial revolution possible, but the legacy of the imperial past in England's contemporary decline. Again, the spectator is enlisted as active discursive partner, sharing subjective responsibility for making connections between the latent nuclei of meanings inscribed beneath the manifest "racial" forms of social conflict. What *Handsworth Songs* does is activate the reality of "social fantasy" in shaping our cognition of the real world: the metaphorical and metonymic logics that cut across the signifying chain of the film-work operate at an unconscious level along the lines of condensation and displacement which Freud identified in the symbolic mechanisms of the dream-work.

"In dreams begin responsibilities," wrote Delmore Schwartz. It seems to me to be crucially important to recognise the multiaccentuated quality of the voices that speak in these new modes of black film-writing because, as Volosinov/Bakhtin pointed out,

> The social multiaccentuality of the ideological sign is a very crucial aspect [of "class" struggle] . . . [as] each ideological sign has two faces, like Janus. This *inner dialectic quality* of the sign comes out fully into the open only in times of social crisis or revolutionary changes.[11]

To the extent that this re-echoes Fanon's insight that the fixed meaning of the signs of colonial authority become increasingly unstable, uncertain and ambivalent at the point where struggles for national/cultural liberation reach a new moment of intensity,[12] the emergence of this quality in black film discourse today implies a qualitative intensification of the struggle to decolonise or de-territorialise cinema as a site of political intervention. The liberation of the imagination is a precondition of revolution, or so the surrealists used to say. Carnival is *not* "the revolution," but in the carnivalesque aesthetic emerging here we may discern the mobility of what Bakhtin called the "dialogic principle" in which the possibility of *change* is prefigured in collective consciousness by the multiplication of social dialogues.[13] What is at issue can be characterised as the critical difference between a *monologic* tendency in black film which tends to homogenise and totalise the black experience in Britain and a *dialogic* tendency which is responsive to the diverse and complex qualities of our black Britishness and British blackness—our differentiated specificity as a disapora people.

> They will be intimately related to the British people, but they cannot be fully part of the English environment because they are black. Now that is not a negative statement . . . Those people who are in western civilisation, who have grown up in it, but made to feel and themselves feeling that they are outside, have a unique insight into their society.
> CLR James[14]

It has been said that the films of Sankofa and the Black Audio Film Collective are influenced and informed by ideas from European artistic practices. Indeed they are, but then so are those films made on the implicit premise of a mimetic theory of representation, whose "neutral" aesthetic dimension bears traces of the influence of the prevailing codes and "professional" ideology of the capitalist film industry, which, of course, is centered in the West. There is no escape from the fact that as a diaspora people, blasted out of one history into another by the "commercial deportation" of slavery (George Lamming) and its enforced displacement, our blackness is thoroughly imbricated in Western modes and codes to which we arrived as the disseminated masses of migrant dispersal. What is in question is not the expression of some lost origin or some uncontaminated essence in black film-language, but the adoption of a critical "voice" that promotes consciousness of the collision of cultures and histories that constitute our very conditions of existence.

We return therefore to confront the paradox, which is that the mimetic mode of cinematic expression is a form of cultural mimicry which demonstrates a neo-colonialised dependency on the codes which valorise film as a commodity of cultural imperialism[15]. The problem of imitation and domination was confronted in literary debates around aesthetics in the African, Caribbean and Afro-American novel in the 1940s, which highlighted the existential dilemma of dependent expressivity: how can the "colonised" express an authentic self in an alien language imposed by the imperial power of the "coloniser"?[16]

There is, however, another response to this problematic, inscribed in aesthetic practices of everyday life among black peoples of the African diaspora in the "new world" of the capitalist West, which explores and exploits the creative contradictions of the clash of cultures. Across a whole range of cultural forms there is a "syncretic" dynamic which critically *appropriates* elements from the mastercodes of the dominant culture and "creolises" them, disarticulating given signs and re-articulating their symbolic meaning otherwise. The subversive force of this hybridising tendency is most apparent at the level of language itself where creoles, patois and Black English decentre, destabilise and carnivalise the linguistic domination of "English"—the nation-language of master-discourse—through strategic inflections, reaccentuations and other performative moves in semantic, syntactic and lexical codes.[17] Creolising practices of counter-appropriation exemplify the critical process of dialogism as they are self-consciously aware that, in Bakhtin's terms,

> The word in language is half someone else's. It becomes "one's own" only when . . . the speaker appropriates the word adapting it to his own semantic and expressive intention. Prior to this moment of appropriation the word does not exist in a neutral or impersonal language . . . but rather it exists in other people's mouths, serving other people's intentions: it is from there that one must take the word and make it one's own.[18]

Today, the emergence of this dialogic tendency in black film practice is important, as it has the potential to renew the critical function of "independent" cinema. Since former generations of black intelligensia have now entered the media marketplace and broadcasting institutions, and some appear to have happily assimilated common-sense notions of "artistic excellence,"[19] the creole versioning and dialoging with critical elements from Euro-American modernism is infinitely preferable to the collusion with the anti-cinematic conservatism inherent in such conformist positions (which continue in the great British tradition of anti-intellectualism).

There is, on the other hand, a powerful resonance between the aspirations of the new work, which seeks to find a film language adequate to the articulation of our realities as "third-generation" black people in Britain, and the critical goals advocated by the concept of Third Cinema which combats the values of both commercialism and "auteurism."[20] Aware of the pernicious ethnologocentric force which Clyde Taylor[21] has shown to be inherent in the very concept of "aesthetics" as such, my aim has been precisely to avoid the construction of a monolithic system of evaluative criteria (itself neither useful nor desirable). Rather, by appropriating elements of Bakhtin's theory I have tried to differentiate relational tendencies in the way black films perform their critical function. Evaluating this function is always context-dependent. The lucid immediacy of *We are the Elephant* (Ceddo, 1987), for instance, not only articulates an incisive account of South African realities of repression and resistance, but in doing so it strikes a dialogic blow against the censorship of image and information-flows imposed by apartheid and the alienating spectacle of money-making epics like *Cry Freedom*. This is to

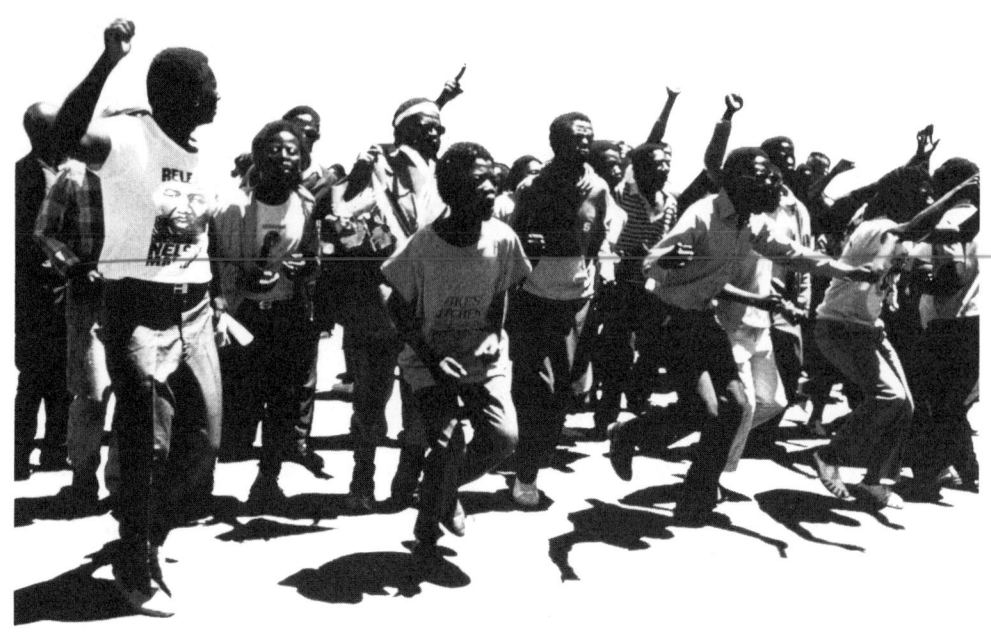

WE ARE THE ELEPHANT

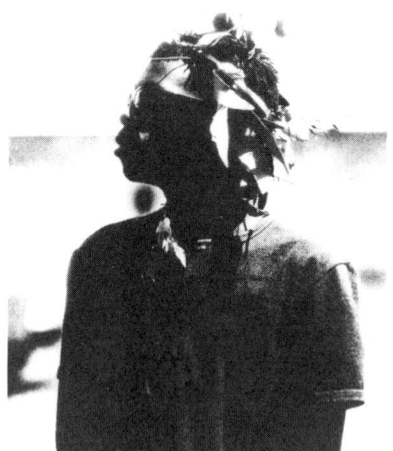

WE ARE THE ELEPHANT: Ceddo Film Video Workshop, Courtesy of: Ceddo Film Video Workshop

say that if there are dialogic moments within films conceived in a conventional mode, there are also profoundly monologic moments in some of the new work, such as the "speaker's drama" in Sankofa's *Passion of Remembrance* and the remorseless repetition of Black Audio's earlier tape-slide *Signs of Empire*. We are dealing not with categorical absolutes but the relative efficacy of strategic choices made in specific contexts of production and reception.

I would argue that new modes in black British filmmaking are instances of "imperfect" cinema, in Julio Garcia Espinosa's phrase[22]: conducting research and experiments, adopting an improvisational approach and hopefully learning from active mistakes through trial and error. In this sense Stuart Hall's comment that the originality of the new work is "precisely that it retells the black experience as an *English* experience," must be amplified. In place of reductionist tendencies in the monologic single-issue approach which creates a binary "frontier-effect" in its political analysis of reality, as if black subjects confront white society as our monolithic Other, critical dialogism gestures towards a counter-hegemonic perspective which assumes that questions of race cannot be isolated from wider social policies. In Hall's terms,

> The fact of the matter is that it is no longer possible to fight racism as if it had its own, autonomous dynamic, located between white people or the police on the one hand and blacks on the other. The problem of racism arises from *every single political development* which has taken place since the New Right emerged.[23]

Critical dialogism overturns the oppositional relations of hegemonic boundary maintainance by multiplying critical dialogues *within* particular communities and *between* the various social elements of the general "imagined community" of the nation. At once articulating the personal and the political, it shows that our "other" is already inside each of us, that black identities are plural and non-unitary and that political divisions of gender and sexual identity are to be transformed as much as those of race and class. Moreover, critical dialogism questions the monologic exclusivity on which dominant versions of national identity and belonging are based.

Paul Gilroy shows how the sense of a mutual and logical exclusivity between the two terms "black" and "British" is an essential condition for the hegemony of racism over the English collective consciousness.[24] New ways of interrupting this hegemonic logic are suggested by the dialogic movement of creolising appropriation.

Fully aware of the creative contradiction, and the "cost," of our outside-in relation to England, cultural work based on this strategy gives rise to the thought that it is possible to turn dominant versions of Englishness inside-out. Gramsci argued that a political struggle enters its hegemonic phase when it goes beyond particular economic interests to make alliances between different classes of the "people" so as to re-direct the "collective will" of the nation ("state + civil society"). On this view, counter-hegemonic strategy depends on the struggle to appropriate given elements in the common sense of the people and to re-articulate those elements of consciousness into a radical democratic direction, which used to be called "equality." At a micro-level, the textual work of creolising appropriation activated in new forms of black cultural practice awakens the thought that such strategies of disarticulation and re-articulation may be capable of transforming the "democratic imaginary" at a macro-level by "othering" inherited discourses of English identity.

Aware that "there is a Third World in every First World and vice versa" (Trin T. Minh-ha), the diaspora perspective has the potential to expose and illuminate the sheer heterogeneity of the diverse social forces always repressed by the monologism of dominant discourses—discourses of domination. In a situation where conservative forces have deepened their hold on our ability to apprehend reality and would have us believe that "it's great to be Great again" (1987 Tory election slogan), we must encourage and develop this critical potential. It might enable us to overcome reality.

FOOTNOTES

(1) Introduction, *Shadow and Act* (New York: Vintage/Random House, 1964) p. xvi.

(2) Reviewing *Passion*, Judith Williamson discerned the influence of Godard, Duras, Mulvey and Wollen; *New Statesman*, 5 Dec 1986. On *Territories*, Colin McCabe found its "visual flair . . . limited by its adherence to the bankrupt aesthetics of that narrow modernism advocated by much of the film theory of the '70s," *The Guardian*, Dec. 4, 1986. Problems of "eurocentrics" in contemporary English critical film-theory are discussed in Robert Cruz, "Black Cinemas, Film Theory and Dependent Knowledge," *Screen* ("Other Cinemas, Other Criticisms") V 26, no. 3-4, May-August 1985.

(3) Novelist Salman Rushdie, born in India and living in Britain, is the author of *Midnight's Children* (winner of the 1981 Booker Prize) and *Shame*. Rushdie's polemic, "Songs doesn't know the score," *Guardian*, Jan. 12, 1987, was followed by letters from Stuart Hall (Jan. 15) and Darcus Howe (Jan. 19).

(4) See, Michael Cadette, "Contrived Passions and False Memories," *Race Today Review '87* (London: V 17, n 4, March 1987).

(5) Cited in David A. Bailey, Introduction, *Ten.8*, no. 22 "Black Experiences," Summer 1986, p. 2.

(6) David Silverman and Brian Torode, *The Material Word: Some theories of language and its limits* (London: Routledge, Kegan and Paul, 1980), p. 6.

(7) "Theses on the Philosophy of History," *Illuminations* (London: Fontana, 1973), p. 257.

(8) See, Stuart Hall and others, *Policing the Crisis* (London: Macmillan, 1979) and Stuart Hall, "The Whites of their Eyes: Racist Ideologies and the Media," in Bridges and Brunt (eds.) *Silver Linings*, (London: Lawrence & Wishart, 1981).

(9) The Notting Hill Gate neighborhood in the London borough of Kensington was an area of mass Caribbean settlement in the 1940s and '50s; scene of the white-initiated "race-riots" of 1958, the first carnival was organized by activist Claudia Jones, and the event has subsequently developed as one of the largest street-festivals in Britain, held annually on August Bank Holiday Weekend.

(10) See, Paul Gilroy, "Stepping out of Babylon—race, class and autonomy," in Centre for Contemporary Cultural Studies, *The Empire Strikes Back* (London: Hutchinson, 1982) p. 300.

(11) V. N. Volosinov, *Marxism and the Philosophy of Language* (New York and London: Seminar Press, 1973) p. 19.

(12) See, "On National Liberation," in *The Wretched of the Earth* (Harmonsworth: Penguin, 1967), and see also Homi Bhabha's introduction, "Remembering Fanon," in the reprint of *Black Skin/White Masks* (London: Pluto, 1986).

(13) See, "Discourse in the Novel," *The Dialogic Imagination* (Austin: University of Texas, 1981, trans. C. Emerson and M. Holquist), and see also, Tvetzan Todorov, *Mikhail Bakhtin: The Dialogical Principle* (Manchester and Minnesota: Manchester University Press, 1984).

(14) "Africans and Afro-Caribbeans: a personal view," *Ten.8*, no. 14, "Black Image/Staying On," Spring 1984.

(15) The imitation of Hollywood form in initial developmental phases of various "national" cinemas is discussed in Roy Armes, *Third World Film-making and the West* (London and Berkeley: University of California, 1987). The transfer of professional ideology is discussed in Peter Golding, "Media Professionalism in the Third World" in James Curran and others (eds.), *Mass Communication and Society* (London: Edward Arnold, 1977).

(16) See, Homi K. Bhabha, "Representation and the Colonial Text" in Frank Gloversmith, *The Theory of Reading* (Brighton: Harvester Press, 1984). These debates have been recently revived in Ngugi wa Thiong'o, *Decolonising the Mind: The Politics of Language in African Literature* (London: John Currey/Heinemann, 1986).

(17) On creolisation and interculturation, see Edward K. Braithwate, *The Development of Creole Society in Jamaica* (Oxford: Oxford University Press, 1971), *Contradictory Omens* (Mona, JA: Savacou Publications, 1974) and on linguistic subversion in the formation of "nation-language," *The Story of the Voice* (London: New Beacon Publications, 1983).

(18) *The Dialogic Imagination*, op cit p. 293-4.

(19) Farrukh Dondy (Commissioning Editor for Multicultural Programming, Channel Four Television) on BBC "ethnic minority" magazine *Ebony*, transmitted Nov. 1986. Darcus Howe and Tariq Ali edit *The Banding File*, a black/Third World current affairs programme, Channel Four.

(20) The concept of Third Cinema proposed by Latin American independent film practice in the '60s—see, F. Solanas and O. Getino, "Towards a Third Cinema," in Bill Nichols (ed.) *Movies and Methods* (London and Berkeley: University of California, 1976)—and subsequently developed with reference to African cinema by Teshome Gabriel, *Third Cinema in*

the Third World: The Aesthetics of Liberation (Ann Arbor: UMI Research Press, 1982), was the focus of the conference held at the 40th Edinburgh International Film Festival (EIFF), 1986. For two versions of this real event see my reflections on "Third Cinema at Edinburgh," *Screen* Vol. 27, no. 6, 1986, and David Will's account in *Framework*, no. 32/33, 1986.

(21) Clyde Taylor's paper "Black Cinema/ White Aesthetics" was presented at the EIFF conference "Third Cinema: Theories and practices" (organised by Jim Pines, Paul Willemen and June Givanni). Dialogic elucidation of Taylor's argument is provided in his counter-reply to Will in "Eurocentrics vs. New Thought at Edinburgh," *Framework*, no. 34, 1987.

(22) See, "Meditations on Imperfect Cinema . . . Fifteen Years Later," *Screen*, Vol. 26, no. 3–4, op cit.

(23) "Cold Comfort Farm" (on Tottenham and Handsworth "riots"), *New Socialist*, no. 32, November 1985.

(24) See, *There Ain't No Black in the Union Jack* (London: Hutchinson, 1987), especially Ch 2. Ch 5, "Diaspora, utopia and the critique of capitalism," provides further clarification of Bakhtin's relevance for thinking a diasporan aesthetic.

THOUGHTS ON NOMADIC AESTHETICS AND THE BLACK INDEPENDENT CINEMA:
Traces of a Journey

Teshome H. Gabriel

I sing
of a man
who was not a tree
but whose roots
spread throughout the land

        Who was not fire
        but who smoldered
        in every blaze
        Who was not water
        but quenched thirst

                I sing
                of a man
                who filled up space
                with his presence
                'cause he was the wind[1]

* * * *

The nomad has been desperately searching for water. He sends his children in all directions. He waits and none returns. His obsession becomes even more violent when his wife, the mother of his children, dies. There appears to be an imbalance in the whole search. He suffers humiliation, pain and agony. It is at this time of extreme gloom that the Goddess of the Sea sends a messenger to him.

The water goddess has remained undisturbed throughout the history of life on the earth. The earth is no more than an island in her world. She has thus remained powerful. Of course, the Goddess of the Sea knows this. She is the primary principle of all existence. While the desert had retained power and authority over living things, it is only water, the maternity of life force, that can defeat it.

Teshome H. Gabriel
Associate Professor
Department of Theatre, Film, TV
UCLA/Associate Director, African
Studies Program

The messenger tells the nomad that the goddess is prepared to send one of her daughters to guide him to the secret site of the legendary spring so he will never thirst again for 1,000 years. But she will thus free him from his search on one condition, and one condition only; that he marry her daughter. The nomad desperately wants water but he also cherishes his freedom of movement. He has been conditioned in his way of life, from childhood, for centuries. If he marries the daughter he knows he will be human-divine and immortal, but if he refuses to marry, he will violate cosmic order. The nomad goes through a deep conflict. He cannot meet the condition of the goddess because it means his desolation.

The nomad is isolated against forces that are more powerful than he. Dejected and confused, sitting around an open fire in the evening, he gazes at the blazing flames and begins to hallucinate about the legendary spring. Suddenly, through the haze there appears a woman that the nomad has not seen before. The woman stands, in darkness. Reaching into the fire, she grasps a handful of glowing embers from the ashes and throws them high into the heavens, their trail of light blazing "pathways to the stars." Ever since, moonbeams and starlight have guided nomads in the night.

On the morning of that night, with a brilliant flash of lightning, the nomad awakens and discovers he has company. A bond of spiritual harmony has been created. The nomad does not know it, but the woman is the daughter of the moon, a niece of the Goddess of the Sea. They have not been heard of since. Some said, they went to the north; others said, they went to the south; still others said, they had been taken to a far away place across the oceans.

"The sky gives witness to history," writes Brenda Marie Osbey in *Ceremony for Minneconjoux*. "Journey with me and see what I see."[2]

"CRANKHANDLES OF HISTORY"

Nomads belong to different cultures. They come from different periods of history.[3] From different time periods, they constantly incorporate and evolve a unique variation of spiritual, artistic and cultural expression. There are as many different lifestyles and aesthetic norms in the nomadic form of social organization as there are cultures and peoples in the world. Nomads are known to be rooted in myth, legend and folklore. Their artistic manifestations in song and dance, ritual and performance, are affirmations of their vigorous association with the earth and its gifts. To them art has two essential factors: (a) the ability to consolidate the community through ritual and performance and (b) collective participation in their dramatized, spoken and artistic forms. By their intensity both in communication and the immediacy of their memory, nomads reflect *par excellence* the lifestyle of a free people.

The impact of their art and their way of life has two important aspects:

1. The fundamental idea that all life, experience and existence is without frontiers or boundaries.

2. The foundational idea of not glorifying fulfillment in terms of territory or resources.

Life of sedentary or settled peoples is mostly controlled by state apparati, codified and written laws, and is dictated by resources which they transform and use. In nomadic thought, all human settlement, related to availability of resources, is only temporary.

Nomads reject the formation of the state because it curtails their freedom of movement; besides, the formation of the state has never been able to fulfill its promises. Nomads have thus developed a way of life, and an aesthetic attitude, which defy and critique both the settlement and art inspired by the state.

The moon is one of the great phenomena that are incorporated in nomadic cultures and that define the transient nature of their art work. The moon has interesting features: it is generous; it has maternal qualities of gentleness. It bathes the nomads after the scorching heat of the sun. The moon also has the capacity of transforming itself—it dies and it reappears every day. The undying moon that is dying. It actually never dies, and it actually dies—which is really the life cycle of human beings written large in the sky. Its reference to the life of the nomadic community is striking. They know they will die but also emerge to life. This is accomplished through ancestoral logic. To the nomads all eventualities become the path—the footprints of the ancestors —upon which the trail of images, signs and "notes of music" are scattered. The instrumentality of these languages expresses free space.

The spiritual life of the nomad is much more highly developed in its co-existensive orientation than that of settled societies. In other words, there is not the same kind of exclusivity between the spiritual world and the physical world. Nor should this be mistaken for fusion between the two entities—the physical and the spiritual world coexist as separate but interdependent features of the universe.

TRAVELLING AESTHETICS

Nomadic outlook also lends itself to a different measure of qualities of artistic expression. In nomadic thought, art has three sides: it has functional, aesthetic and spiritual dimensions. One side of this triangle never rules out the others. Inextricably linked with this notion of art is the concept of reality.

1. Reality and Fantasy

In nomadic thought, "reality" is both tangible/seeable and untouchable/unseeable. What is not necessarily seeable and touchable, but which nevertheless exists, is merely an extension of known reality. Although the supreme reality is the earth, what is beyond or absent from this reality is explored through and manipulated by a system of fantasia. This is less anchored on symmetric or tangible realities; it subscribes to an inverted reality utilizing memory and experience to recreate the ephemeral qualities of existence. First, the cosmos is experienced and recalled as a fantastic phenomenon and then transformed—inverted—into an accessible and tangible reality through art, dance and ritual.

In short, the perceived entities of reality—i.e., the moon, the stars, mountains, wind, sun or oasis—assume a highly symbolic order. Hence, the most fantastic, sophisticated poems are in fact metaphoric structures and systems of multifaceted representation. In nomadic thought, the fantastic, which is a direct extension of everyday life, merely represents a heightened experience. In this kind of system, other planets or other words are no more than an exaggeration or minimalization of an otherwise known reality. This differs from Western metaphor, in which systems of fantasy are dislocated from reality and deviate from the known structure of homo sapiens.

The nomadic view is that the spiritualized entities and the realities of human existence are fused together, in an interactive creative relationship, creating a balance between the earth world and the sky world. The coexistential perceptions of these entities simultaneously evolve a symbolic world order which defies separateness, segmentation and isolation. In this instance, something is always present and absent at the same time. For the nomad, experience is not separated or segmented into categories of functions and aesthetics. In nomadic thought, what is specific (the aesthetic experience) is at the same time homogenous (i.e., it is part of an integrated experience of the mind), and vice versa. Here, aesthetic satisfaction corresponds to an aesthetic energy that the nomad consumes from physical entities that make him alive.

To nomads, art tells stories from experience and from memory. It cannot be simply one or the other; the two must coexist, as do the two worlds and two qualities of phenomena.

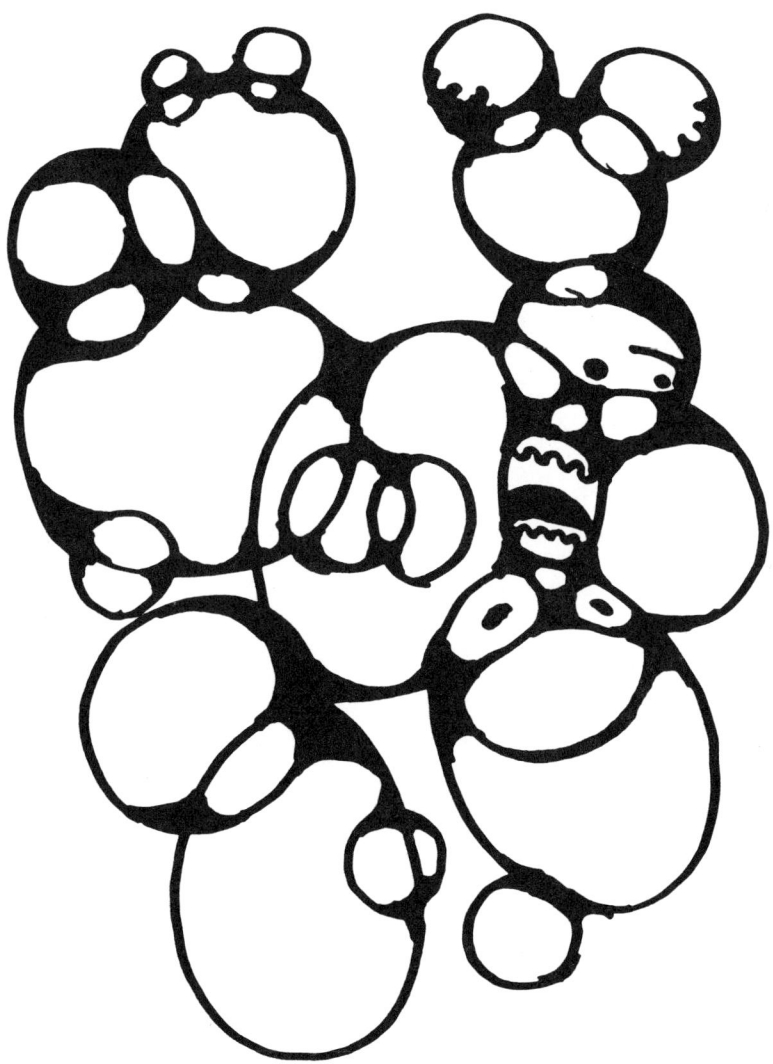

Illustration by: Mahammod Issa

Thus, their world and their aesthetics are more detailed and scorpious in manifesting ceaselessness, vastness and limitlessness in scale and temporal quality. These are manifest in three different ways:

I. Art defies closure,

II. Art rejects the structural model of beginning, middle and end, and

III. Art reflects a cosmic integrity in the realms of (re)presentations.

2. *Temporality/spaciality*

In the Western context, time assumes its own "objective" existence. It is equated with the individual and is measured according to production output. Because time is measured in production, people are invested in units of time. Time is perceived as an investment and is thus valued more than the actual actors/participants in production. Time is narrativized into discrete elements of past, present and future. What issues from this is an intellectual and artistic justification for a way of life that validates a certain philosophy, and a certain tendency in modernism.

In nomadic orientations, units of time are far more broad. Time is seen, observed and experienced as "subjective." It arises out of observed and experienced relationship between planetary bodies. The central orientation points toward a "cyclic" system wherein several time frames occur simultaneously. In this kind of conceptualization, greater store is put on the value of actors/participants in production. Time does not control people, but people tend to operate within flexible time frames. In nomadism, time is not abstracted; it is an outcome of experience—it arises from life itself.

Space exists because there are tangible phenomena which are seen and felt. But there are also objects/phenomena that are touchable and seeable that we do not see that fill up space. The conception of space is thus relative to seeing, feeling and touching. To settlers, living in close proximity, distance and space are turned into an abstraction, into a greater introspection. We thus know less about more, and nomads know more about less. For instance, they have several words for village, environment and livestock. They also have a very keen sense of vision and sound. They smell the rain before the fall; they hear and see clearly where others distort. We see water where they see only mirage.

To nomads, time and space are both subjective phenomenon, operating within the system of the local absolute. The absolute is a matter of social consensus—it does not make any difference if it is, or is not. The important aspect is that there *is*, or there exists, an absolute against which to measure relationships and values of things, actions, ideas and so on.

Western systems glorify the Abstract in conceptions of Time and Space. Western thought has a love-hate relationship with the Absolute. If and when it is applied, it is abstracted and takes the notion of *the* Absolute. Take, for instance, Da Vinci's "Mona Lisa." We are told to admire the beauty of the painting for its enigmatic quality. We are told that what accounts for the painting's enduring quality is the smile. But beauty is invested in values and not in time.

In Western conceptions of the Mona Lisa, the desire to concretize and seal these values as timeless and as an Absolute is presented in detailed and scientific manner. So much is suggested and so little revealed. That which is (ir)rational seems to necessitate the voice and expression of the many volumes written about it.

Subjective nomadic time prescribes that Mona Lisa's smile and beauty is ever shifting—OK yesterday, so today and tomorrow who knows—it depends on circumstances of everyday feelings and experiences. To the nomadic way of thinking, Mona Lisa is tentative, incomplete, arbitrary, temporal and relative. In nomadic thought, everything is subject to aging. There is nothing timeless or enduring about beauty or aesthetics. It is, therefore, best to characterize the notion of asthetics as transient or travelling.

* * * * *

Nomads in Quotations:

"I'm from a nomadic society," Mahamood Issa said. "They make art, but they don't consider it as art. When two nomads meet in conversation, while one talks, the other will take a stick and design in the sands. They would be talking, I would be watching the design . . . Then an hour later, they would be gone, the design would be gone, the art would be gone."[4]

* * * * *

"The more I read, the more convinced I became that nomads had been the crankhandle of history, if for no other reason than that the great monotheisms had, all of them, surfaced from the pastoral milieu . . ."[5]

* * * * *

"Legend has it," writes John Berger, "that Pyrrhon, the founder of scepticism, was at first a painter. Later he accompanied Alexander the Great on his voyage through Asia, gave up painting and became a philosopher, declaring that *appearances and all perceptions were illusory*." [emphasis added][6]

* * * * *

"It is the women who make us live in the desert. They say the desert brings health and happiness, to them and to the children."[7]

—Sheikh, Sidi Ahmed el Beshir Hammadi of Mauritania

* * * * *

Brian Massumi, in his Forward to *A Thousand Plateaus* wrote:

> The "nomads" whose thought lies behind the work of Deleuze and Guattari—Lucretius, Hume, Spinoza, Nietzche, Bergson—are united by no school or direct lines of influence, only by their critical relation to official philosophy and its historical complicity with the state. They are also secretly linked, in Deleuze's words, by "the critique of negativity, the

cultivation of joy, the hatred of interiority, the exteriority of forces and relations, and the denunciation of power."[8]

And what did Deleuze and Guattari say?

In an altogether different way, in a totally different context, Arab architecture traces a space which begins very near and very low, placing the light and airy below and the solid and heavy above. This reversal of the laws of gravity turns *lack of direction* and negation of volume into constructive forces. A nomadic absolute exists in the form of a local integration that proceeds from one part to another and constitutes smooth space as an infinite succession of linkages and changes in direction. It is an absolute identical with becoming itself, with process. It is an absolute of passage, which in nomad art merges with its manifestation. Here the absolute is local, precisely because place in undefined.[9]

* * * * *

And what did Ib'n Khaldoun say?

The Desert People are closer to being good than settled peoples because they are closer to the First State and are more removed from all the evil habits that have infected the hearts of settlers.[10]

"You cannot travel on the path before you have become the Path itself."

—Guatama Buddha

* * * * *

In a film, *Memory and Future*, by the Colombian filmmakers Marta Rodriguez and Jorge Silva, an Indian woman says, "I think, even if one dies, one doesn't lose its memory."

* * * * *

Ignatieff: Let me see if I understand this. Human beings originate on the desert plains of Africa three million years ago . . .

Chatwin: Yes . . .

Ignatieff: . . .and they gradually acquire a set of instinctual behaviours that enable them to survive on the grasslands and vanquish their predators . . .

Chatwin: Yes . . .

Ignatieff: . . .and as they acquire a set of instinctual nomadic patterns of behaviour they also acquire a meaning system, a set of myths which are imprinted on the brain over millions of years . . .

Chatwin: Yes . . .

Ignatieff: . . .and these are the story patterns that keep recurring even in the modern day.

Chatwin: Absolutely.[11]

* * * * *

"I wonder how people remember things who don't film, don't photograph, don't tape . . . The new Bible will be an eternal magnetic tape of a Time that would have to reread itself constantly, just to know it existed."

—Chris Marker in *Sans Soleil*

* * * * *

And what is the visual model for "time immemorial"—towards which everything is direction and from where everything springs?

* * * * *

"It suits me to make pictures on celluloid . . . memory pictures . . . that make stories more interesting and exciting. With film, you are able to transpose these pictures of memory, imagination and reality, and make a [visual] story from them. It is, I think, a continuation of the oral tradition. That's how I see my work."[12]

—Merata Mirta

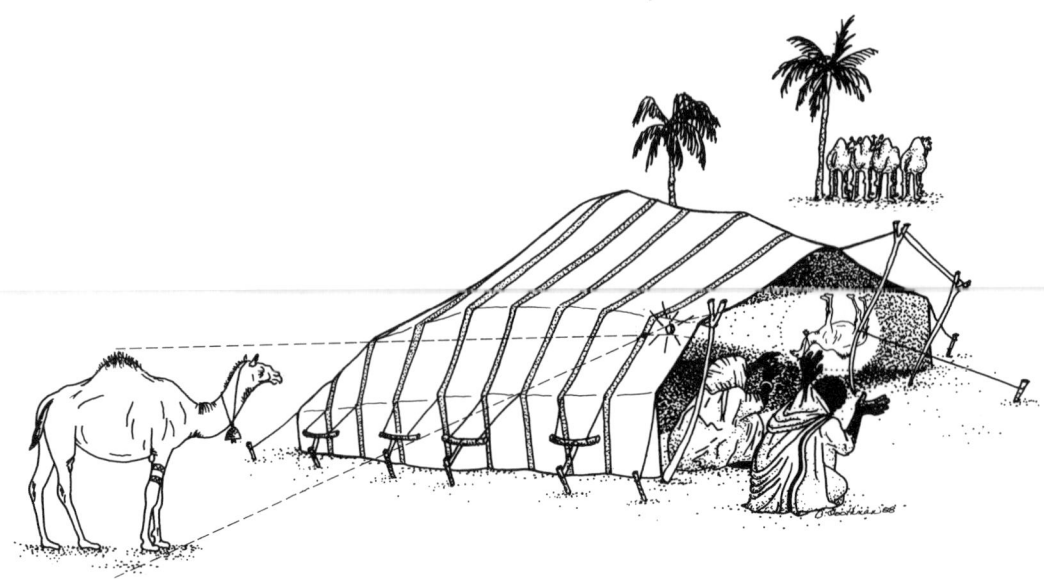

To us it is Da Vinci's camera obscura (16th century); to the nomads perhaps it is Ibn Al Haytham's optics (10th century) Illustration by: Nancy Toothman

BLACK CINEMA/TRAVELLING CINEMA

In my research for an alternative aesthetics of black independent cinema, I came across no man's land—to an oasis of wilderness, to the nomads in the desert. Today, nomads, in the book of travels, are to be found in the Americas and in the genesis of myths which reach back to the African savannah. Whether they are the San, Nam, Barwa Bathwa of the Kalahari, the Bedouin of Arabia, the Bakhtiaris of Persia or the Somalis and Fulanis of East and West Africa, or the Eskimos and the Indians of North and South America or the Originals (Ab-origines) of Australia, all reach back to "Africa" where the first human cry was heard.

Though black people and nomads may be racially and ethnically distinct, Language, in the broadest sense, unites them. The dominant aspect of this language is symbolism, metaphor, music and performance. They are also united in the very idea of space—they are both marginalized and (de)territorialized peoples. To both, collective memory, rather than official history, is of crucial importance. To both memory evokes mosaic images and sounds, and invades everyday existence. Both reject the idea of closure or termination, be it in their artistic manifestation or in their lifestyle. Just as the nomads are synthesizers of surrounding cultures they pass through, so are the blacks. They live in the industrialized world, but they do not belong to it; they pass through. Both opt not to adopt but to adapt. They incorporate some aspects and not others. Both seem not to be governed by the idea of physical home as much as by the mythical and spiritual home that they cherish in their belief systems and carry in their cultures. Both are obsessed by the very essence of freedom.

Black filmmakers break constraints and cross borders; they are not oppositional but pro-active in their creative work. They create their own aesthetic terms in film discourse. Call them ethnobiographies, film essays, film poems, film lore or a combination thereof: they incorporate "in clear rhythm with Africa" long-term memories and heritages. Herein are some examples from the archeology of black cinema:

In the genesis of black independent cinema the very titles of the films read like vocabularies from a nomadic dictionary. *Passing Through* by Larry Clark, *Black Exodus* by Iverson White, *Passion of Remembrance* and *Territories* by Isaac Julien and Maureen Blackwood, *Ashes and Embers* by Haile Gerima, *Patu* by Merata Mita, *Handsworth Song* by John Akomfrah, *Bless Their Little Hearts* by Billy Woodbury, *Burning an Illusion* by Menilik Shabazz, *King Carnival* by Horace Ove, *Langston Hughes: Dream Keeper* by St. Clair Bourne, *Pathway to the Stars* by Antonio Ole, are all examples that illustrate the terminological leitmotif of nomadic cinema and the lexicon of Nomadic philosophy.

Ben Cauldwell's *I and I*, which has its origins in African mythology, is an allegorical and metaphoric search for black identity. Barbara McCullough's *Water Ritual* is an act of purification on a spiritual and mythic level. Haile Gerima's *Bush Mama* is a film with floating style on life in the ghettoes of Industrial America. Julie Dash's *Illusions*, part one of a four part series, *Bridges*, is on the conflicts of dual identity of the African-American. *A Different Image* by Sharon Larkin is a search that traces the features of an African identity. All these films carry aspects of nomadic sensibility even if the filmmakers themselves are not aware of it. We can therefore understand why when Charles Burnett, maker of the *Killer of Sheep*, was asked; "How did you make this masterpiece of realism?" he replied, "I don't know, I just got raw stock and shot the film."[13]

And from other parts of Africa and the Third World a similar tendency abounds; we have *Ceddo* ("The Outsiders") and *Emitai* ("God of Thunder or Death or God of the Sky") by Ousmane Sembene, *Barravento* ("The Turning Wind") by Glauber Rocha of Brazil, *The Promised Land* by Miguel Littin of Chile, *Wend-Kuuni* ("God's Child or Gift") by Gaston Kabore of Burkina Faso, *Naitou* by Moussa Kemoko Diakite of the Republic of Guinea, and many others carrying aspects of travelling aesthetics.

Nor are all forms of Western filmmaking ignorant of nomadic aesthetic. Perhaps most noteworthy in this regard is Chris Marker's *Sans Soleil* in its sensitivity to non-western cultures and its self-acknowledged (in)ability to penetrate them.

> "My personal problem was more specific: how to film
> the ladies of Guinea Bissau?" says Chris Marker,
> " . . .the built-in grain of indestructibility of
> African women. . . . I see her—she saw me—she knows
> that I see her, but just at an angle where it is
> still possible to act as though it was not
> addressed to me."[14]

So too, Akira Kurosawa's *Dersu Uzala*, allowing its identification to influence its very aesthetic form, succeeds in communicating a sense of the nomadic, not only in its story but, perhaps more importantly, in its spacial aesthetics and in its formulation of the title character's relationship to nature. As if by acknowledgement of its nomadic impulse, one striking shot of the film shows the moon and the sun in the sky at opposite ends of the screen. Perhaps nowhere else in Western cinema has one single image more adeptly captured the essence of nomadic sensibility.

1. *The Journey Theme*

In black films there is often the depiction of journeys across space or landscape. Viewed as a whole, a pattern seems to emerge around the journey theme: wandering, exile, migration and homeland. Journeys acknowledge encounters with others, with known and unknown forces, happy or horrendous. Whatever themes these films carry, or whatever the land(e)scape they traverse, these do not seem to be the important aspect. The land ceases to be mere land, and only exists as a kind of mythic wilderness.

The journey is the link(age); without it there is no film. There is no film in and of itself. A film by itself is therefore meaningless—it conveys nothing. Film exists so that the journey may exist, and vice versa. Of course, the story sets the travel from place to place. But it is not important in itself. All filmic phenomenon is subordinate in importance to the voyage. And the trace is more significant than the point of contact. Film is simply a foreshadowing device with allusions to memory. One cannot film without one's shadow. Film is only the siren call of the road: this is one of the key principles of nomadism.

2. *Axis and not Poles*

One of the limitations of mainstream theory and criticism has been its tendency to see the cinematic movements as tied to one of two poles: dominant (Hollywood) and oppositional (reactive) cinema. Typically, Hollywood and similar practices are lumped into the former, while Third World and independent movements are associated with the latter. This is problematic because it fails to recognize what are in fact the merging tendencies of alternative filmmaking such as those which are here described as nomadic.

Thus, even in critical writings, Hollywood has been seen as a purveyor of colonial discourse and as a betrayer of others' cultural values. Understood merely as oppositional, black independent cinema could not be seen but as a reactive cinema. However, black independent cinema's search has gone far beyond this, for it is in fact a search for a newly born cinema, one with its own discrete identity, evolving on its own axis. It must be understood as more than a reactive pole—but rather as the development of new, emergent tendencies which are more difficult to categorize in established norms. Oppositional filmmaking is, in and of itself, not an axis; rather it is one of two opposite poles. It thus has no self-identity. Its films make use of the same reference and language of exploitative cinema.

To try to define black independent cinema merely in terms of otherness is also to create merely another reactive pole. Theorists of otherness fail to take into account that otherness speaks the same language of oppositional cinema. Culture and cinema are heterogenous and multiple and need not and cannot be fitted to a hierarchical model. To succumb to the notion of the other is to be a part of the same, to be trapped within the confined and prescribed boundaries that limit it. The other is always that which Western culture

excludes in order to exploit.

Working within the debris of culture and discourse, black independent cinema moves not in between the two opposing poles but around it towards its own axis. Here the authority of the margins is born, in those blind spaces where the hierarchy of oppositions do not hold complete sway, where language confounds itself, and where liberated culture resides. In those liberated spaces outside of Hollywood and oppositional cinema, a new, newly born cinema is emerging, a cinema not-yet-here but no-longer-there, a travelling cinema—nomadic cinema. It is only in open free spaces that a new cinema can both deconstruct and construct this cinema. It is only through work of nomadic sensibility that black cinema, independent, feminist, exile and Third World cinema will capture its axis. That is why an authentic black cinema cannot be but a new, newly born, post-cinema, with new reality. We are thus witnessing a time when one cinema is dying and another one is being born in its place.

We can thus understand why Glauber Rocha remarked, "If we think that Hollywood is dangerous for us, so is Sartre [as Hegel, and others], and very much so." He added, "it's better to have a form that's badly polished but new."

* * * * *

NOTES ON NOMADIC CINEMA

Virtually from the beginning of cinema, with very few exceptions, the modes of genre classifications and styles have never been blended. Nomadic cinema brings an unprecedented and unexpected jolt to cinematic reality by smashing down boundaries—between documentary, ethnographic, travelogue, experimental and narrative fiction. Nomadic cinema makes both habit and virtue of this jolt.

1. *The Mask as the Screen*

In nomadic thought, one wears the mask during festivities to summon the universe to existence and put the world in motion. The mask represents the Absent one. It brings the unknown to recognition, the unrepresentable to representation. The mask itself is an object, it is abstract; yet it indicates that the content is present in the abstraction—where the known becomes unknown, the identical becomes different. The unrepresentable and unknowable is always "the missing content," that the mask recovers and brings forth. The mask puts the world upside down—it is a masquerade.[15]

The Screen is like the painted mask. Spectators put on the screen to sing a world into existence in movie-houses. The screen is worn at dusk, and the mask at dawn. The screen tends to distort reality and disguises meaning, while the mask de-frames the world, in inverted order, not to conceal, but to heighten and add significance. The "missing content" of the screen is "ideology," while that of the mask is "spirit." In both, there is an exchange between absent-present and between representable-unrepresentable, except that with the screen, one does not control it; "meaning" is spelled out to us; we have no contact with the screen; it does not have the social/collective aspects of the mask. There is no social boundary with the mask. Here, spectators have relation to it. Briefly, we summarize the difference as follows:

Mask	*Screen*
Spirit	Ideology
Collective memory	Official history
Long-term memory	Short-term memory
Interactive mode	Isolative mode
Social/collective relation	Individual relation (social is myth)
Spectator represents himself	Spectator does not represent himself
Significance: spectator makes his/her social connection	Meaning: spectator is given a social meaning, the world is him/her
Un-framed	Framed

The screen frames the world right side up. It limits its scope. It frames the world for the consolation of the turbulent viewer, who is excluded from representation. The screen, the spectacle, masks reality as a facade—the image of reality scoffs at reality itself. The screen serves as the canvas on which the West paints its own stereotypes of others. Social/collective relations to mask and the memory behind them give beleaguered cultures a strength which outlasts the brute forces of colonial culture. Therefore, to view the screen, the spectacle, more like a mask, a ritual, is to restructure one's viewing habits, i.e., to interact more socially, both with the screen and other members of the audience.

Nowhere have we seen this more clearly in American movie houses than in the screenings of Spike Lee's film, *She's Gotta Have It*. Is it any wonder that the film was roundly received by viewers, despite its clearly sexist overtones? Three elements, common to nomadic aesthetics, perhaps account for this: (a) its strong sense of place (New York's Bedford-Stuyvesant ghetto); (b) its use of face-to-face address to the audience (in the tradition of oral discourse); and (c) the resulting interactive mode which is obtained both between the film and its audiences, and among audience members themselves. Thus, the viewing experience becomes more than simply a relationship to a screen—it becomes a happening, an event.

2. *Aesthetics as woman*

As a branch of philosophy and theory, aesthetics itself is problematized by nomadic expression. A wandering life produces a wandering aesthetics. A traveling aesthetic requires traveling theory and criticism; yet theory and criticism are canonized, and thus become a way of fixing rather than liberating their objects. Nomadic practice thus creates havoc for such an orientation. Intrinsic to the nomadic mode of expression is an ever-constant shifting of its form and content and the relationship among them and their audience.

In theoretical and critical writings of the past, Third Cinema has been offered as one way to contextualize such aesthetics, giving it its liberatory due. To this we wish to add that these aesthetics are in fact tied closely to the mythical figure of the woman. The nomadic epic, at its best, is thus truly a woman's epic. By this it is meant that within the context of these nomadic travels what has been emphasized are various mythic and symbolic images of maternity, referring back to the land (Mother Earth) and water (Goddess of the Sea), which provide our sustenance and existence. Thus, the concept "female" represents that which both nurtures humankind and that which inspires and engenders aesthetic expression.

3. *Towards a Poetics of Nomadic Aesthetics*

Aesthetic is always outside the work; it is extra-cinematic. Its definition, its appreciation, its survivability are determined by the receiving subject, the spectator's memory, daily whims and fancies. Images in a film thus belong to the past; they represent re-mini-scen(c)es. However, though images belong to the past, they carry simultaneously possibilities and promises, because they also belong to the future. A nomadic cinema, then, is:

A cinema with a ritualized styles,
    with a theme that hovers between
        the reasoned action of psychological reality and
        the inspired action of memory and forgetting.
A cinema of celebration rather than tension.
A cinema with a long-ago time frame,
    with an unbroken action,
    followed through in long takes.
A cinema freed from story and linear structure.
A cinema where sound and image vary by the movement of the
    wind.
A cinema that floats over reality.
A cinema that is able to break the logic it sets up for itself.
A cinema that defies its own progress toward closure.
A cinema that creates a rupture of its own expressive form.
A cinema of anxiety, of ideas and mythic place.
A cinema produced cinematically and contextualized culturally.
A cinema with unrushed wholeness that imparts stature and
    dignity.
Where the hero's welcome is, at best, tentative.
    Where off screen, the filmmaker berates his actors
    about the reasons he is making the film.
Where the subjects snap back that they are
    merely the script treatment.
Where black-frames interrupt process as discussions ensue.
Where the filmmaker finally walks into frame, to reflect on his ambivalence between
    —resolving the conflict with his actors, and
    —to ruminate his commitment to complete the film.

This shows how film itself becomes part of alienation in filmic discourse. But the rupture and its acknowledgement are redeeming. The stylistic rift incurred becomes a specific part of the discourse. Nomadic cinema takes into account whatever is outside of the intended idea or script. This cinema resists opting for one mode exclusively. Through the use of a transgressive style, this cinema stresses, yet minimizes, conflict. It is a cinema of emphasis, of process:

A film that acknowledges itself conceptually.
A film that "traces no counters and delimits no form."
A film that is comfortable with readings that float.
A film that "both attracts spectators and allows them no place
    to rest."
A film where the prefilmic proves to be hopeful rather than
    accurate.
A film that is elated at being "a particle, a sprout," an unfinished song.

CARNIVAL OF REMEMBRANCE

Along the coastline of Rio de Janeiro and Salvador in Bahia, every year, during the Summer Solstice (when the sun's eclipse is at the furthest north and south of the equator), Brazilians of African descent and others celebrate for an entire day in song, dance, ritual and carnival, in homage to Iamanja, the Goddess of the Sea. And when the sun sets "above the waves," and the moon awakens "above the clouds," all the celebrants face towards Africa, and in remembrance of an ancient homeland, throw flowers and gifts to the Goddess of the Sea:

> Your holy spirit floats
> along the cresting waves of the water,
> as we walk out upon the sands,
> night time closing on the longest day of the year,
> and join together in small circles
> around the sacred boats
> that we shall send you,
> each whispering our prayers to a flower
> that we lay upon the boat,
> for Iamanja, Holy Queen Sea.[16]

And all the roads branch out freely into all directions, to land and to sea. There are no longer boundaries to be patrolled. We are back in the African Savanna, and into several chains of sand dunes, plains and forests. We have entered into Africa of the Africas, we are in Angola:

> I sing
> of a Man
> who was not a myth
> 'cause he was the land

>   Who was in Ebo
>   and who did not bend
>   in Kifagondo
>   but who held
>   high the banner
>   and he was
>   a stout imbondo vine[17]

Here are the footprints from the not-so-ancient past. How momentous a whisper to a seed, and "prayers to a flower," can be. Here is the mask of memory—an anthem for Travelling Cinema—drawn from a poem by the heroic nomad-warrior, Agostinho Neto:

Following
    the pathway to the stars
along the agile curve of a gazelle's neck
above the waves above the clouds
on springtime's wings of camaraderie

A simple note of music
an indispensable atom of harmony
a particle
a sprout
color
in the multiple combinations of humanity

Exact and inevitable
like the inevitable past of slavery
within our consciousness
like the present

Not abstract
without color
    amidst colorless ideals
without odor
    amidst the odorless rain forests
    of rootless trunks

But real
clad in green
in the fresh smell of forests after the rain
in the vigor of thunder and lightning
hands sustaining the germination of laughter
above the fields of hope

Eyes filled with freedom
ears with sound,

    of avid hands on drumheads
in rapid and sharp rhythms
of rivers Zaire deserts Kalahari mountains light
made crimson by endless fires
    in the violated grasslands
spiritual harmony of tom-tom voices
in clear rhythms of Africa

This is
    the pathway to the stars
along the agile curve of the gazelle's neck
on to the harmony of the world.[18]

Footnotes

(1) A poem by the Angolan poet and militant, Arnaldo Santos. The myth that follows the poem is my own construction.
(2) Brenda Marie Osbey, *Ceremony for Minneconjoux*, Callaloo Poetry Series, University of Kentucky Press, 1983.
(3) I am thankful to Prof. Mazisi Kunene, the distinguished South African poet, for an illuminating discussion on nomadic cosmology.
(4) "Ex-Somalian Exhibits 'Versatile' Art," *St. Louis Post-Dispatch*, October 15, 1987.
(5) Bruce Chatwin, *The Songlines*, (New York: Elisabeth Sifton Books, Viking, 1987), p. 19. I am indebted to this work for its inspiration.
(6) Special issue on The Story-Teller, *Granta*, #21, Spring 1987, p. 18.
(7) Chatwin, p. 178.
(8) See #9.
(9) Gilles Deleuze and Felix Guattari, *A Thousand Plateaus*, trs. by Brian Massumi, University of Minnesota Press, 1987, p. 494. See also, "Nomad Art" by Deleuze and Guattari, *Art & Text*, #19, 1985. Deleuze and Guattari's work has been particularly useful and inspiring in this study.
(10) Chatwin, p. 196.
(11) *Granta*, pp. 29, 30.
(12) Interview with the Maori filmmaker Merata Mita, *Framework*, #25, June, 1984, p. 3.
(13) Monona Wali, "The Invisible Cinema," Los Angeles *READER*, February 24, 1984, p. 15.
(14) The entire text of Chris Marker's narration, "Sunless," appears in *Semiotext(e)*, Volume 4, Number 3, 1984.
(15) For an interesting discussion on "Art and Masquerade," see *Art and Text*, #19, Oct.-Dec. 1985, pp. 47–52. See also Roland Barthe's *Camera Lucida*, trs. by Richard Howard, Hill & Wang, New York, 1981, pp. 34 & 35.
(16) Merlin Stone, *Ancient Mirrors of Womanhood*, Beacon Press, 1979, pp. 96 and 97.
(17) This is a continuation of the first poem cited by Arnaldo Santos. Incidentally, the entire poem is written in memory of Agostinho Neto, First President of Angola.
(18) This poem, by Agostinho Neto, is recited in the film *Pathway to the Stars*. The film is patterned after the poem.

PARTIAL LIST OF MATERIAL CONSULTED:

1. "*Niger's Wodaabe: People of the Taboo,*" *National Geographic*, Vol. 164, No. 4, October 1983, pp. 483–509.
2. *Nomads, Exiles, and Emigres*: The Rebirth of the Latin American Narrative 1960–1980, Ronald Schwartz, The Scarecrow Press, Inc., Metuchen, N.J. 1980.

3. *Black Arts and Black Aesthetics*: A Bibliography by Carolyn Fowler. Atlanta University, Atlanta, Georgia, 1976.

4. *Black Aesthetics*: Papers from a Colloquium held at the University of Nairobi, June 1971. Editors: Pio Zirimu and Andrew Gurr, East African Literature Bureau, Nairobi, Kampala, Dar Es Salaam, 1973.

5. "The Politics of Exile," a special issue of *Third World Quarterly*, Vol. 9, No. 1, January 1987.

6. *Blank Darkness*: Africanist Discourse in French. Christopher L. Miller, Chicago, University of Chicago Press, 1985.

7. *Black Face Maligned Race*: The Representation of Blacks in English Drama from Shakespeare to Southerne. Anthony Gerard Barthelemy, Louisiana State University Press, 1987.

8. *Nomads of the World*, published by The Special Publications Division. Ed. Rob. L. Breeden, The National Geographic Society, 1971.

9. *Pioneers & Settlers*: the Aboriginal Australians. Catherine H. Berndt and Ronald M. Berndt, Pitman, Australia, 1978.

10. *Veiled Sentiments*: Honor & Poetry in a Bedouin Society. Lila Abu-Lughod, Berkeley, University of California Press, 1986.

WE DON'T NEED ANOTHER HERO:
Anti-Theses on Aesthetics

Clyde Taylor

Blacks in the diaspora have largely forgotten their connection to the familiar African dilemma of needing to sift and mediate progressive directions from the options of tradition vs. techno-capitalism—perhaps because this choice has been forced on them over a longer historical stretch and under different conditions. Out of this search Afro-modernity arises, the transformation of the best traditional values in the post-feudal context of industrial society, and the simultaneous extrication from the co-products of western industrialism: slavery, colonialism and imperialism. The fine work of separating Afro-modernity from "modernization-westernization" is linked to the greater need to make an epistemological break from the seductions of first-world ideology. This imperative is felt most profoundly as the project of cultural decolonization. Those who work to build black cinema, or in other media of representation, connect with this project at an advantageous point by first making a break from the repressive doctrine of aesthetics.

Aesthetics, which is, of course, synonymous with western aesthetics, was concocted in the 18th century as an instrument of ideological control for the comfort of the first-world ruling class. Its principal injury to its class victims lies in its doctrine of the autonomy of cultural production and appreciation. Through this specious paradigm, it appropriated knowledge of human creativity for the interests of one social sector, alienating those outside the western bourgeoisie from their own creativity and the socio-political knowledge embedded therein.

Aesthetics demands resistance both to its philosophical/ critical dogmas and to the discursive practices that rely on its traditions, canons and genres. For where aesthetic practise, or aestheticization, manifests, often brilliantly, the human creativity that is demonstrably distributed everywhere, this particular mediation of that creativity is not innocent. None of its forms, techniques, rules or cultivated expectations are free of ideological purpose. This is also true of any transindividual symbolic order. Were aesthetics not as a doctrine destructive to the cultural orientation of black people, grounds would remain for resistance because of the imbalance of discursive power challenged by demands for a new world information order.

As a practise, the mischief of aestheticization is seen at work in William Styron's novel, *The Confessions of Nat Turner*. There, lyrical prose, deft characterizations, moving descriptions, etc., at first distracted many black readers from its reduction and trivialization of an awesome black historical figure, thereby obscuring and reductively rewriting Turner's own more powerful and entirely different autobiographical account of himself, even to the point of usurping the title of Turner's memoir.

Out of the decolonizing eruptions of the 1960s the Black Aesthetic appeared as one of the dialogues challenging the hegemony

---

Clyde Taylor Associate Professor
Department of English
Tufts University

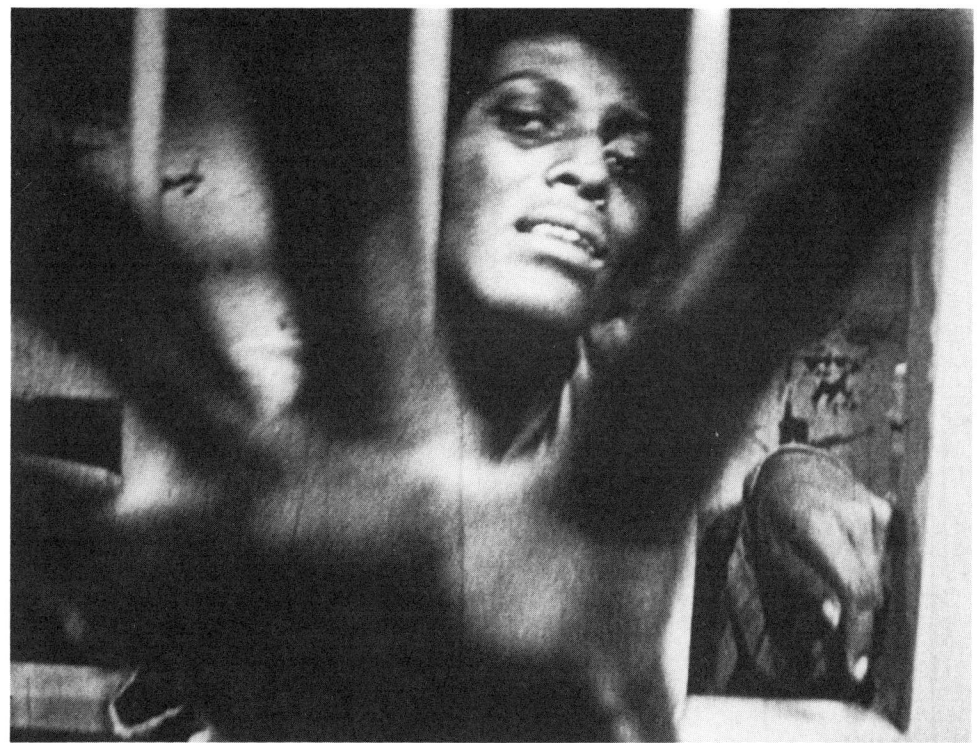

CHILD OF RESISTANCE: Haile Gerima, courtesy of: Mypheduh Films

of aesthetics. It produced a vital, necessary redirection within liberative thought. If it is presently losing its force and momentum, it is partly from the difficulty of recognizing from the beginning that all aesthetics are western. (Let every culture define its own creative practise!)

The Black Aesthetic sprang from the Black Arts Movement and largely follows the description set out by Larry Neal: "The Black Arts Movement is the cultural arm of the Black revolution." The misleading influence of aesthetics is visible in this semi-autonomous conception of cultural production apart from social and material production. This self-concept of the Black Arts Movement, which reproduces the separate aesthetic realms of first-world institutions, surrendered vital dimensions of economics and politics to others. The ambiguous political posture of the Black Aesthetic in recent years grew

out of this truncated self-concept.[1] The arm has lost touch with its revolutionary body. In the Age of Reagan, Thatcher and Botha, the Black Aesthetic has modulated into a genteel pursuit of black academic accommodation. Thus neutralized, the Black Aesthetic is now nearly compatible with neo-conservative black literary criticism, while recent movements toward a black film aesthetic build on the accommodating formalist grounds of oral narrative, folklore and griotology—important, valid, but necessarily rear-guard contributions to the decolonization project.

After the groundwork of the Black Aesthetic, the conditions of possibility exist for a more incisive break from normative culture through development of postesthetic creative practise and interpretation. Postesthetics extends beyond the cultural particularism of ethno-aesthetics to interface with the revisions in knowledge posed by feminism, class analysis and some of the dissidents of postmodernism. From a position outside its sphere of influence, aesthetics is revealed as an obstruction in the path of cultural reintegration of black people. The critique of aesthetics opens a reexamination of the whole question of representation.

All knowledge is representation. And every representational sign or image bears one face that expresses (and perhaps also hides) a cultural-ideological allegory. In the rhetoric of representation, asserts Sylvia Wynter, "feelings are constituted." The personal references of inner speech, once transliterated into public signification, become contestants for a place in discourse within mythologemes and ideologemes, which is to say within knowledge. The cultural-ideological face of the given sign determines the way the power of that knowledge will be measured, used and contested. In postesthetics, the relation of a sign to the discourses of power and resistance becomes primary.

The question arises, since old habits die hard, what the character might be of critical interpretation of black cinema or other representations from a postesthetic perspective. Rather than offer another formula to replace those of the aesthetic regime, postesthetics proposes a reorganization of knowledge around, and by means of, the given text. Initially, postesthetic discourse is no more remarkable than the many public utterances in, say, film reviews and journalism, where a given text is discussed without recourse to the mystifications of aesthetics. Yet, lacking specific markers of resistance, such discussions are "naturally" assumed to fall into the comfortable lap of liberal humanism.

This problem has preoccupied many cultural sign-shapers— writers, filmmakers, artists—who have devised strategies to face it. Postesthetic practise can be located in scattered quarters. Blacks working in any past era to dispel the mythologies of dominance have made renovations from which postesthetic reconstruction can profit. The fiction and non-fiction of Richard Wright reflect an awareness of this problem, as do the writings, films and discussions of Ousmane Sembene. Fictive works such as Alice Walker's *The Color Purple*, the novels and essays of Ishmael Reed, Haile Gerima's film *Child of Resistance* and Melvin Van Peebles's *Sweet Sweetback's Badaaass Song* show specific efforts to break out of the prisonhouse of aesthetic discourse.

A deliberate instance of postesthetic reconstruction has been given us in *The Other Francisco*, by Afro-Cuban filmmaker Sergio Giral. Here a classic tale of slavery, romanticized and aestheticized, is deconstructed and then reconstructed through a more pragmatic social analysis. Postesthetic analysis is embedded in the cultural and music essays of Amiri Baraka, the decolonization writings of Fanon, Sylvia Wynter, Ngugi and Chinweizu, and in such critical texts as W. Lawrence Hogue's *Discourse and the Other*, H. Bruce Franklin's *The Victim as Criminal and Artist*, Jim Pines's *Blacks in Films* and Donald Gibson's *The Politics of Literary Expression*. Resistance to "western aesthetics" is pronounced among Black Aestheticians and black women writers (see the interviews in *Black Women Writers at Work*, edited by Claudia Tate).

Postesthetic critique recognizes the need to reclaim and reorganize these rebellious concepts of representation from aesthetic discourse, as liberated territory. For postesthetics has an important role to play in constructing paradigms for the assembly of counter-knowledge. It attempts to bring structuring force to the discourse of resistance. It seeks, in the greatest possible explanatory power brought to bear on social relations, an avenue toward progressive self-empowerment. It aims towards paradigms structured enough to

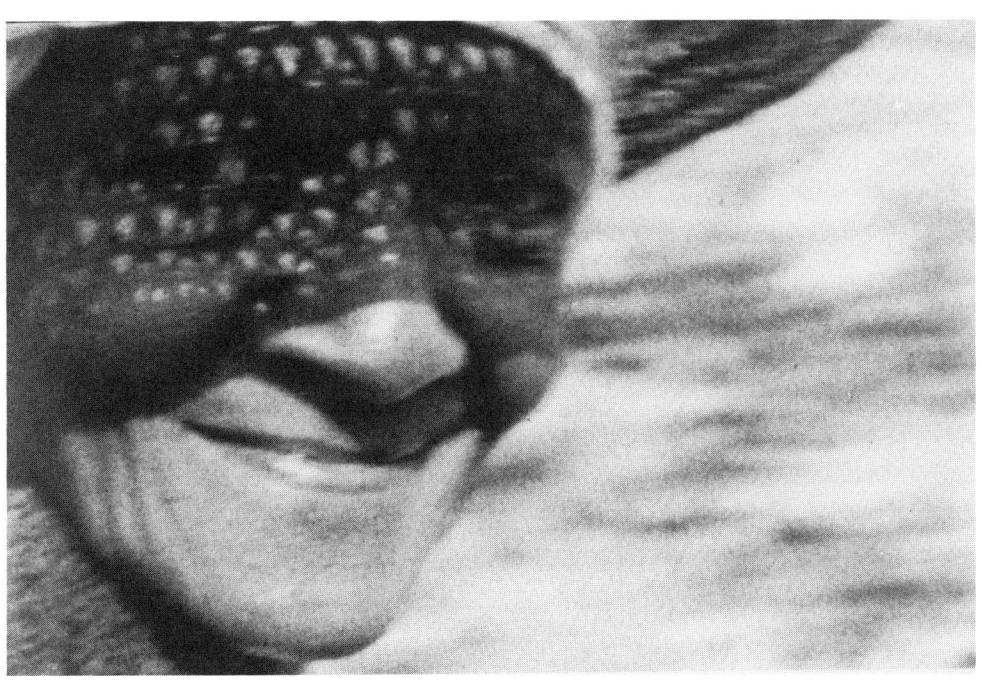

ASHES AND EMBERS: Haile Gerima, courtesy of: Mypheduh Films

maintain a perpetual engagement against symbolic hegemony, but without the dogmatism that would repress the heterogeneity of liberated, democratic expression. By contrast, the accumulable force of the very divergent works mentioned above would probably escape the analytical instruments of the Black Aesthetic.

In postesthetic interpretation the individual text is freed of specious autonomy. Instead the text is opened to intercommunication with other texts and to the significations of everyday life. The object of a perfected, rounded interpretation of a work viewed in isolation becomes irrelevant. Yeats's dilemma, whether to perfect the life or the work—a typical conundrum of aesthetics—is easily resolved from a postesthetic standpoint in favor of the life, with whatever help the work can give it. The aim in postesthetics is to seek satisfaction from the production and exchange of liberating knowledge, not the pleasure of the text. The individual text is viewed as the site of competing inscriptions of knowledge. As such it may contribute to the accumulating vocabulary of postesthetic critique through negative or positive illumination, or both.

With the text of representation now open to the range of social articulations, postesthetic critique sees the need to renounce the boundaries established by the aesthetic-cultural hierarchy, such as those between film and literary studies. It values socio-political over formalist interpretation. It does not merely "draw on" other disciplines such as the sociology of knowledge, media studies, history, cultural studies; it perceives particular themes from these and other fields as constituents of its paradigm. And in the course of its textual analyses in, say, film criticism, it aims for mutually productive dialogue with other efforts to revise the languages of knowledge, such as popular history, reconstructive Black Studies and reconstructed world history.[2] In the same spirit it violates national boundaries in its attempts to reintegrate cultural and historical analysis.

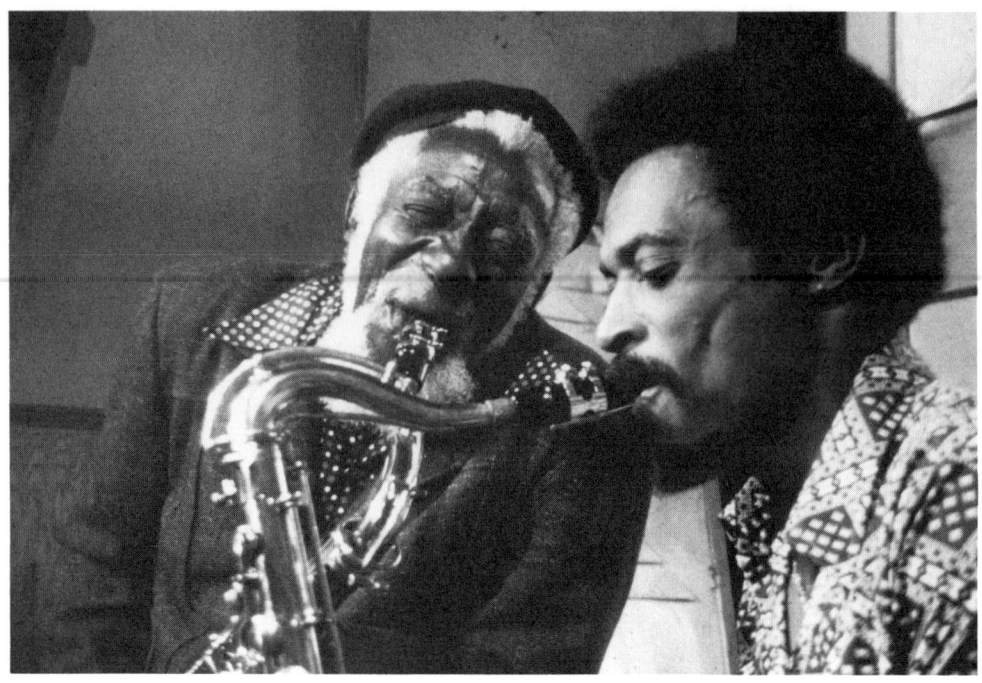

PASSING THROUGH: Larry Clark, courtesy of: Larry Clark

Postesthetics represents an effort to revivify and validate meanings dismissed or obscured in imperial knowledge. Hence a major commitment of postesthetic analysis is the process of transcultural and transideological recoding by which meaning and explanatory power are recouped from dominant paradigms. To be sure, every social exchange in some small measure rewrites the character of social relations. But in postesthetics, focal attention is given significant recodings which promise to add to the store of counterknowledge. One major construct of progressive black recoding was embodied in the shift in self-designation from *Negro* to *Black*. And in cinema we can observe Haile Gerima's *Ashes and Embers* recoding the representation of the disoriented black war veteran travestied in Hollywood's movie *Home of the Brave*. Or we can profit from the socio-informative gains in Sembene's recoding in *Black Girl (La Noire de . . .)* of the conventional representation of the black maid-servant registered in *Imitation of Life*. Gerima's *Bush Mama* decolonizes and recodes the representation of the black welfare mother otherwise glamorized in *Claudine*. *The Wedding of Mariamu* re-images the traditional African healer and in so doing exposes the reflex regularity with which Hollywood glosses all black non-canonical spiritual belief as ignorant superstition or voodoo demonry. *Sweetback* decolonizes the sign of the wild black stud, rendered as Crown in *Porgy and Bess* and recolonized in *Sparkle*. Larry Clark's *Passing Through* reinscribes the black musician as serious cultural voice after the aestheticization and trivialization of *Paris Blues* and other Hollywood jazz films. Alile Sharon Larkin's *A Different Image*, in title and text, recodes and amplifies the reference of black women in popular representation.

The dance of signs recoded and re-recoded into the protean shapes of knowledge never ends; it is an inescapable fact of language. The Black Aesthetic became lulled into quietude by its fascination with images of perfect and static essences. The "post" in postesthetics acknowledges its platform for the assemblage of reconstructive knowledge as inevitably transitory, to be surpassed, let us hope, by more powerful and humane modes of explanation. But for this historical moment, postesthetics brings to black cinema a perception of its cultural practises as a crucial site of the contest out of which the human is being rewritten. If progressive intellectuals are arrogant enough to attack the drugging of the people through mass culture, they should be prepared to go cold turkey in quitting their own addictions to the opiates of aestheticism.

FOOTNOTES

(1) Harold Cruse's *Crisis of the Negro Intellectual* (1967) registers a dense warning against the social cost to black self-empowerment from the separation of considerations of culture, politics and economics.

(2) See Raphael Samuel, ed., *People's History and Socialist Theory* (London, 1981); *Introduction to Afro-American Studies* 2 vols. (Peoples College Press, P.O. Box 7696, Chicago, IL 60680); *Radical History Review*, no. 39, issue devoted to "Structures and Consciousness in World History" (September 1987).